# THE
# MEANING OF
# METALLICA

# THE
# MEANING OF
# METALLICA

*Ride
the Lyrics*

## WILLIAM IRWIN

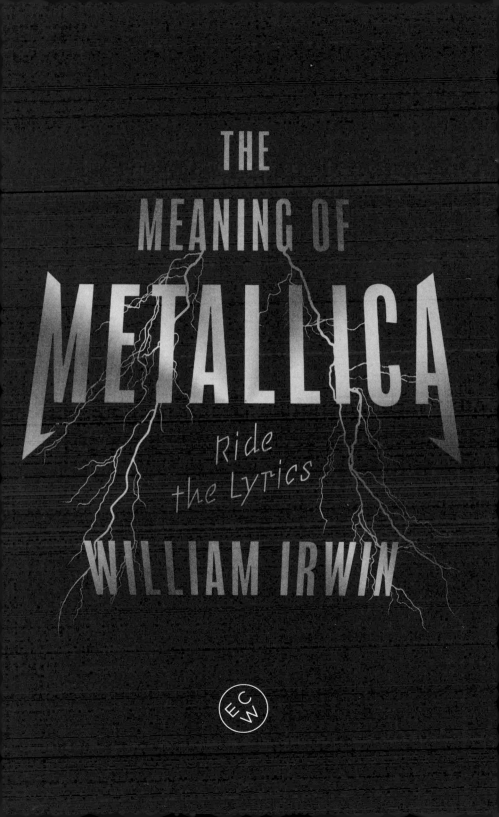

Copyright © William Irwin, 2022

Published by ECW Press
665 Gerrard Street East
Toronto, Ontario, Canada M4M 1Y2
416-694-3348 / info@ecwpress.com

Editor for the Press: Michael Holmes
Cover design: David A. Gee

LIBRARY AND ARCHIVES CANADA CATALOGUING IN
PUBLICATION

Title: The meaning of Metallica : ride the lyrics /
William Irwin.

Names: Irwin, William, 1970- author.

Identifiers: Canadiana (print) 20210356235 |
Canadiana (ebook) 20210356243

ISBN 978-1-77041-618-5 (softcover)
ISBN 978-1-77305-919-8 (ePub)
ISBN 978-1-77305-920-4 (PDF)
ISBN 978-1-77305-921-1 (Kindle)

Subjects: LCSH: Metallica (Musical group) |
LCSH: Rock musicians—United States—
Biography. | LCSH: Heavy metal (Music)—
United States—History and criticism. | LCGFT:
Biographies.

Classification: LCC ML421.M587 I79 2022 | DDC
782.42166092/2—dc23

PRINTED AND BOUND IN CANADA

PRINTING: MARQUIS     5  4  3  2  1

# CONTENTS

# THE ECSTASY OF GOLD

I n 1984 my friend Joe taped his *Ride the Lightning* LP for me. In 1986 I saw Cliff Burton play live. In 1987 I paid $5.98 for *The $5.98 E.P.* In 1994 I reluctantly cut my Metalli-mullet. Those are my fan credentials. You may go back further with Metallica, or you may have found the band more recently. Metallica fans like to claim OG status, but it doesn't really matter. What matters is what Metallica has meant to you. I wasn't there from the beginning with Metallica, but they were there from the beginning for me—the beginning of my struggle within. I am now 52 years old, and Metallica has provided the soundtrack of my life since I was 14. But this book is not about me. It's not even about what Metallica has meant to me.

This book is about the lyrics of James Hetfield. Some fans focus on the music and don't pay much attention to the words. I'm not one of them. Fans like me believe Hetfield's lyrics are worthy of the same attention that Bob Dylan's receive. As a folk singer, Dylan was recognized as a serious writer from the beginning of his career. By contrast, as a metal musician, Hetfield has not yet received his due for the profundity of his lyrics. This book aims to remedy that situation. Metal fans know that our favorite music provides plenty of food for thought. Yes, the worst of the genre is mindless noise, made merely for commercial gain, but that is true of nearly any genre. More than 80 percent of popular recordings concern romance, and most are trite. Hetfield's lyrics stand in stark contrast, dealing with death, war, addiction, alienation, corruption, freedom, religion, and other weighty topics. In the few songs that focus on love, Hetfield gives us much more than sweet "Cherry Pie." Most popular music is just entertainment, something to dance to, something to party with. Metallica's music is real art, something to experience, something to contemplate.

It's bold to claim that this book is about *the* meaning of Metallica. For one thing, the book focuses on Hetfield's lyrics. Meanwhile, the music may have its own meaning beyond, or in addition to, the words. For another thing, Metallica is a cultural phenomenon that transcends their music. It means something to be a Metallica fan, to be devoted to the band, to have an opinion on the controversies, to feel a sense of community with other fans. This book does not attempt to do justice to that kind of meaning. Perhaps most importantly, Hetfield's lyrics mean different things to different people. For each of us who has listened closely and thought deeply, the lyrics have distinct personal significance. That kind of individual relevance is priceless, but it doesn't always translate well when talking to other people. So this is not a book about what Hetfield's lyrics mean "to me." Occasionally, I include a personal reference, but only when it helps to paint the bigger picture of what a particular song is about. Likewise, occasionally I discuss how the music reinforces the lyrics.

In addition to the general significance of the songs, the meaning we're after in this book is the meaning of the lyrics as Hetfield intended. I don't claim to know that meaning with certainty, and I have not interviewed Hetfield to get him to tell me. It's not clear that he would always have fully settled answers anyway. For songwriters, lyrics sometimes start without a plan. A phrase or a line comes to the songwriter with a melody, and more is built on that foundation. Hetfield seems to write the lyrics for most songs after the music, and his words display the kind of craftsmanship that shows they have been scrutinized and revised in the composition process. Even if the initial inspiration for a lyric comes without a plan, it is kept with a commitment that solidifies into an intention. It would be fascinating to know more about Hetfield's composition process and the genesis of certain songs. Where possible, I have made use of interviews in which Hetfield has spoken about specific songs. But, like most songwriters, Hetfield is often cagey and plays things close to the vest. This makes sense because the songwriter's personal inspiration and personal attachment to a song are not always pertinent to what he intends the song to mean and how he wants the audience to understand it.

Still, it is tempting for fans and critics to play detective and interpret songs in light of what we know about the songwriter. This is fair, but we must often stop short of attributing the views in a song to the songwriter. Hetfield writes and sings the lyrics for Metallica, but often he is giving voice to the point of view of a character. That character may be speaking in the first person as "I," but that does not necessarily make him Hetfield. The speaker in the song is the narrator. Sometimes we may be on safe ground in saying that Hetfield himself is the narrator, but not always.

In dealing with narrators, we are treating Metallica songs like the poetry they are. This book will not get into rhyme schemes and poetic meter or any of the shit that might have turned you off from poetry in the past. Instead we'll be looking at the play of words and ideas, the way Hetfield uses imagery and metaphor to excite our curiosity and tell his stories. Rock poetry works well only when you know the music. The lyrics are meant to be heard along with the instrumentation, not read on their own. So I hope that when I quote Hetfield you hear his voice in your head as it pierces through the music. This is a book aimed at fans, but non-fans should find it accessible (even if they can't hear the music in their heads). The chapters are structured around themes, and the mashup subtitles of the chapters hint at some of the songs discussed. There is thematic overlap for some chapters—you can't fully isolate the themes of war and death, for example. A natural progression leads from one theme to the next, but readers should feel free to skip around and read the chapters in whatever order they want.

I don't claim or aim to have the final word on the meaning of Metallica. Far from it. Fans have been discussing the meaning of Metallica's songs in basements, barrooms, and backyards since the 1980s. And starting in the 1990s the internet connected Metallica fans across the world, facilitating friendly, and sometimes not-so-friendly, discussion. I hope this book catalyzes further discussion and brings more serious attention to Metallica.

No doubt, you'll find places where you disagree with my interpretation. Here's my e-mail address: williamirwin@kings.edu. And here's my Twitter handle: @williamirwin38. I'd love to hear from you. This book is just the beginning.

But now the lights have gone down, and "The Ecstasy of Gold" is playing in the background. So let's get started.

# CHAPTER 1

# RELIGION

*The Creeping Leper Messiah that Failed*

By writing about religion James Hetfield exorcised personal demons from his childhood in Downey, California. Virgil and Cynthia Hetfield raised James in the Christian Science church, a denomination that prohibits modern medicine. Hetfield's father taught Sunday school and was particularly zealous. Meanwhile James witnessed such sights as a young girl giving praise for how the Lord had healed her broken arm, even though anyone could see that it was now mangled.

Despite devotion to his faith, Virgil abandoned his family when James was 13. Three years later James's mother, Cynthia, died from cancer after refusing conventional medical treatment. James had no choice but to move in with his older half-brother David in nearby Brea, California. No more church for James, at least not for many years. His anger at his parents and his knowledge of the Bible proved potent, though. Whereas other metal bands embraced faux-Satanism to shock and scorn, Metallica steered clear of such clichés. Thanks to

Hetfield's subtle descriptions and reflections on what he had seen and read, a series of songs starting with "Creeping Death" thoughtfully critiques religion.

"Creeping Death" was inspired by scenes from Cecil B. DeMille's epic film *The Ten Commandments* (1956). The song tells the story of the tenth plague, the death of the firstborn, largely from the perspective of an angry God, seeking vengeance against the pharaoh and the Egyptians for enslaving his people, the children of Israel. The opening verse sets the stage: "Slaves / Hebrews born to serve, to the pharaoh / Heed / To his every word, live in fear / Faith / Of the unknown one, the deliverer / Wait / Something must be done, four hundred years." One-word lines punctuate this verse and others, allowing Hetfield to hit points of emphasis.

The first word of the song, "Slaves," is startling. The tone with which Hetfield snarls the word could be mistaken for anger directed towards slaves. But the second line quickly clarifies that the song will be about slaves who themselves are angry and certainly have an angry God on their side. The second line also tells us right away who the slaves are, the Israelites. It goes without saying that the life of a slave was terrible; "fear" does not do it justice. Nonetheless, the Hebrew people have "faith"—another one-word line—in the God of their fathers, the patriarchs: Abraham, Isaac, and Jacob. Why, though, does God wait 400 years to liberate them? The brothers of Joseph did wrong, acting out of jealousy and selling him into slavery, but are the sins of the father really to be visited upon the sons? For how many generations? From a human perspective, 400 years of slavery does not seem like a fair punishment for what some ancestors did, especially considering that the descendants of Joseph, the brother sold into slavery, were among those who were enslaved.

**THE MEANING OF METALLICA**

The genius of "Creeping Death" is that without being explicit, it raises questions about God's justice and about the rationality of believing in such a God. The story is told in such a way that we sympathize with the Hebrews and root for the vengeful God, but then afterward we are left to reflect and wonder about the justice and rationality of this God. It is the stuff of fantasy fiction, yet the story comes straight out of the Bible.

Consider the ambiguous line "Faith / Of the unknown one, the deliverer." Does it refer to God or Moses or both? As the biblical story goes, Moses has a life of privilege until he becomes upset when he sees an Egyptian striking a Hebrew slave. In the spirit of vengeance, Moses kills the Egyptian and is forced to flee. Over time, Moses becomes the unlikely leader of a slave rebellion. In a sense, he, in his faith, becomes "the deliverer." So is God perhaps "the unknown one"? Largely forgotten by the Israelites over the course of 400 years of slavery, this God will now make his presence felt. The narration shifts several times in the song, with God himself voicing certain sections, as when he says, "Now / Let my people go, land of Goshen / Go / I will be with thee, bush of fire." The instruction to "let my people go" occurs in several places in the biblical text, including Exodus 8:20, where God tells Moses to deliver that message to the pharaoh. Thus God does not speak directly to the pharaoh. The "land of Goshen" was the area of Egypt inhabited by the Hebrews, from which they departed, and the "bush of fire" refers to God's appearance to Moses in the form of a burning bush that was not consumed by flames. In this form, God gave the order to Moses to lead his people out of Egypt. God promised to be with them, but not in the form of the burning bush. Rather, as the biblical story goes, God led the people as a pillar of cloud by day and a pillar of fire by night.

The verse continues, "Blood / Running red and strong, down the Nile / Plague / Darkness three days long, hail to fire." Egypt was warned in advance about the first plague, that the river would turn to blood and the fish would die. According to the Bible, though, the pharaoh was unimpressed with the plagues because his magicians could duplicate them. Thus the plagues did not seem like ample evidence that the God of the Hebrew slaves was powerful enough to warrant their release. The lyric "hail to fire" is not a call to worship, but rather a description of the seventh plague in which hail and fire (in the form of lightning) struck the land and killed people and animals. In *The Ten Commandments* the hail ignites into flames when it strikes the ground. The lyric "darkness three days long" refers to the frightening ninth plague, in which a "darkness that can be felt" descended upon Egypt for three days. Apparently, even that was not enough to scare the pharaoh into freeing the Hebrews.

Actually, the pharaoh considered freeing them more than once, but, as the biblical story goes, God repeatedly hardened the pharaoh's heart such that the ruler did not give in to his own inclination. The question is: Why did God intervene in this way? The pharaoh hadn't done anything awful by the standards of the time and place. Slavery was common practice. In the Old Testament, God does not forbid slavery—just the enslavement of one Hebrew by another. So it seems that God wanted to demonstrate his power and exercise his prerogative by taking his revenge. With the pharaoh's heart hardened, and maybe his brain blocked, the stage was set for the most dreadful plague, the tenth and final, the death of the firstborn.

The chorus begins, "So let it be written / So let it be done." It's a pronouncement that sounds straight out of the Bible but which actually comes from the film *The Ten Commandments*.

And in the movie it is Pharaoh Sethi speaking (later echoed by Ramesses II). In point of fact, the book of Exodus does not mention the name of the pharaoh. This is one among many reasons that scholars do not think that the story is historical. In addition, there is no Egyptian record of a slave rebellion anything like the one we find in the Bible. Nonetheless, "So let it be written / So let it be done" sounds perfect in the song, as if coming from the mouth of God. The pharaoh has been forewarned with nine plagues already, so he has sealed his own fate. The verse continues, "I'm sent here by the chosen one," and the final line reveals the identity of the narrator: "I'm creeping death." Cliff Burton reportedly described the eerie killer mist in the film as "creeping death," lending a lyrical hand to Hetfield.

The song's narrator claims to be sent by "the chosen one," but that is an odd name or description for God. The Hebrews are, or become, God's "chosen" people. They agree to worship only him, and he agrees to be their protector. The people are chosen, and Moses in particular is chosen by God to be their leader. So is Moses the chosen one? Perhaps, but Creeping Death says that he is sent by the chosen one, and Moses doesn't actually send the tenth plague. God does. Moses is just the messenger. Perhaps God is the chosen one. Though God never calls himself that in scripture, the description fits in the sense that God is chosen by the Hebrews. Long before the Exodus story, Abraham chose to follow the one God. And in the desert, after fleeing Egypt, the Hebrews will accept a covenant whereby they commit themselves to the worship of the one God and the observance of his laws.

The upshot is that on this interpretation, the narrator, Creeping Death, is separate from God. His task is "to kill the firstborn pharaoh son." Indeed, he will kill all firstborn Egyptian males. Thankfully, the young Egyptians do not die a violent death. Instead, they simply go to bed and fail to wake the next morning. But imagine the horror across the land, as mothers shriek upon the discovery of the lifeless bodies of their babies. A rare but real phenomenon, crib death, or Sudden Infant Death Syndrome (SIDS), strikes fear in the hearts of new parents. The cause is unknown, but the baby simply stops breathing overnight. Creeping Death seems a suitable name for crib death.

In fact, another Metallica song, "Enter Sandman," was originally inspired by SIDS, though during the writing process the song morphed into dealing with an older child who says his prayers, actually making it an even better fit for the tenth plague, which killed not only infants but all firstborn males. "Enter Sandman" includes the world's creepiest child's prayer. With each line repeated, the version in the song goes: "Now I lay me down to sleep / Pray the lord my soul to keep / If I die before I wake / Pray the lord my soul to take." This child's bedtime prayer dates back to the 18th century, a time when children died in far greater numbers than they do today in the developed world. Nonetheless, it is a scary prayer, acknowledging the fact that the child may die in his or her sleep. The prayer hung on a placard in my room as a kid in the 1970s, and I was certainly disturbed by it. In the Metallica song, the Sandman is transformed from the benevolent creature who sprinkles sand in your eye to bring pleasant dreams into the malevolent creature who brings nightmares and perhaps death.

"Creeping Death" continues with a ferocious verse as the eponymous agent of death sings, "Die by my hand / I creep across the land / Killing first-born man." In live concert performances, particularly in the 1980s, the audience participation during this part was chilling, with hordes of angry young people repeatedly chanting "Die!" That sense of identification is indicative of the song's ability to enlist the sympathies of early Metallica fans who felt oppressed (by parents, teachers, priests, bosses, or whomever) and lusted for revenge. Anyone unfamiliar with the ritual might have been scandalized at the sight and sound of thousands of young people chanting "Die!" The effect for the participants, though, was cathartic, a purging of negative emotions rather than a catalyst for negative actions.

The phrase "by my hand" is curious. Part of the song was written by Kirk Hammett and performed as "Die by His Hand" in Hammett's previous band, Exodus. Creeping Death, whatever it is exactly, does not have hands. So we need to take "by my hand" metaphorically. It means that he's doing it himself and very personally. Visually potent, "by my hand" invokes an image of a ghostly grip strangling the life from children as they sleep.

As in the first verse, the final verses are punctuated with single-word lines: "I / Rule the midnight air / The destroyer." With a blaring "I" Hetfield barks the point of view of the narrator, Creeping Death. The claim to "rule the midnight air" fits the biblical story and appeals to the listener. In addition, crib death tends to strike between midnight and 9 a.m., and the deaths of the firstborn Egyptians took place overnight. The power of the line, though, derives from the audience identification. The angry young people to whom the song first appealed certainly liked to think of themselves as in charge after midnight. During the hours when authority figures slept, young people ruled. Creeping Death calls himself "the destroyer," again a fitting image for the song and for the audience. In the first book of the Bible, Genesis, God is both the creator and the destroyer, creating the world in six days and destroying it in a flood. In the second book of the Bible, Exodus, God is a destroyer of the Egyptians in order to create a new nation of Israel.

"Creeping Death" effectively enlists the sympathies and identification of the audience who want to act out the role of the destroyer vicariously. With a novel or film we may identify with a character and root for him, but with a song we can identify all the more deeply by singing along and taking the point of view of the narrator. The fan who sings along to the record or the live performance is empowered by the first-person declaration that "I / Rule the midnight air / The destroyer." *I* rule, and *I* am the destroyer. Destruction is much easier than construction, though. Hetfield creatively constructed the song, an act of empowerment. By contrast, the fans singing along imagine destroying something or someone.

The song continues, "Born / I shall soon be there / Deadly mass." The single-word line "Born" is jarring. Who is born? We know, but the answer is left as an unspecified second person. You, the Egyptian (not the listener), are born. What happens next? "I shall soon be there." It sounds like a benevolent promise to rescue or protect, but we know it is anything but that. The phrase "deadly mass" may be inspired by the film's depiction of the plague as a deadly mist, but we can make a religious connection by seeing Creeping Death as enacting a "deadly mass." The Catholic mass is a ritual reenactment of the Last Supper of Jesus, which itself was the annual Passover meal commemorating this very night from Exodus. In the Catholic mass the sacrifice of Jesus is recreated and participants eat the body and drink the blood of Jesus in the form of transubstantiated bread and wine. Jesus is the lamb of God who takes away the sins of the world. In the Exodus story, liberation comes when the death of the firstborn Egyptians, including the Pharaoh's son, finally convinces the ruler to free the Hebrews. In the New Testament, the sacrifice of Jesus is supposed to be done out of love, with God giving his only begotten son to atone for the sins of humanity. By contrast the sacrifice of the "deadly mass" is done out of vengeance, punishing the Egyptians for enslaving the children of Israel.

Again, the song invites identification with the lines, "I / Creep the steps and floor." A sinister scene and presence is painted, even more haunting than in the film. The powerful agent does not need to be stealthy, but he nonetheless derives pleasure from the ability to wreak vengeance undetected. The identity of Creeping Death is again unclear. Is it God or a separate agent of God? At the very least, God seems to identify with his agent much as the listener identifies with the first-person narrator. After creeping the steps and floor, he brings "final darkness." Recall that the ninth plague had brought three days of literal darkness to the land of Egypt. Now metaphorical darkness, death, will swallow the firstborn sons.

The song's next line is a single word, "blood." Significantly, in the first plague, the Nile had run red. Blood remains unseen when all is well. By contrast, grisly loss of life comes with bloodshed on the battlefield, and vampires silently sip the stuff from the necks of their victims. The targets of Creeping Death lose no blood, however. Instead the life drains from them without a mess. We get the explanation in the concluding lines: "Lamb's blood painted door / I shall pass." In the biblical story, God gives elaborate instructions for how every Israelite family is to slaughter and sacrifice a lamb. The blood of the lamb is then to be applied to the Hebrew houses so that God will "pass over" and spare the lives of the firstborn males inside. The story is celebrated and commemorated to this day in the Jewish holiday of Passover. Likewise, the story's imagery was co-opted by Christian theology to enshrine the crucifixion of Jesus, the lamb of God. We who drink the lamb's blood and eat his body in the form of communion will be wiped clean of sin and spared from damnation.

It is a powerful story, rich with symbolism, both in the Jewish original and the Christian sequel, but it raises puzzling and disturbing questions. For one, why did God need the Hebrews to apply the blood to the doors of their houses in order for God to know which ones to pass over? Wouldn't an all-knowing God recognize the houses of his people without such a barbaric marking? He would have no reason to kill the firstborn sons of his chosen people, so they had no reason to feel particularly grateful for being passed over. In general, it is an unflattering portrait of God, and without exaggerating the details of the biblical story, the Metallica song shows us how nasty this God is. He let his chosen people be enslaved in Egypt for 400 years, and when he decided to liberate them he hardened the pharaoh's heart so that the ruler resisted and the Lord had an excuse to wreak vengeance. This God seems a long way from the all-loving, all-knowing, all-powerful God of modern belief. But that is as it should be. The Old Testament never claims that God is all-loving, all-knowing, and all-powerful. Yes, he created the world and is very powerful, but he has his limits. This is the God of a tribal people from the Iron Age.

What's more, there is little, if anything, historical about the account. Egyptian records bear no trace of a massive slave rebellion or any mention of the Israelites. Archaeologists have combed the Sinai Peninsula in search of evidence of such an exodus and have come up completely empty-handed. Nearly all scholars agree that the story of Exodus was written in the sixth century BC during the Babylonian exile, drawing on existing oral and written traditions. While the Hebrew people lived in Babylonian captivity, they wrote a founding myth, according to which they had once (centuries before) been slaves in Egypt, where God freed them from bondage. Thus the story inspired hope that the Israelites would one day be freed from their Babylonian captors, and indeed they were.

Although "Creeping Death" exposes God as a nasty character, one perhaps unworthy of belief outside the Iron Age, the song nonetheless makes God seem cool. Like Tony Soprano, the God of "Creeping Death" is a bad guy we root for. It doesn't matter that God is harsh and unfair in his treatment of the Egyptians. The Hebrews have been enslaved, and so we naturally extend our sympathy to them. We identify with them because we feel oppressed. Who doesn't feel oppressed to one extent or another? Especially the teenagers to whom the song first appealed—never mind that most had life pretty good in retrospect. On their own, the Hebrews are unable to throw off the chains of oppression. Only a supernatural force can save them. It is the stuff of heavy metal fantasy, and so we sing along and pump our fists in the spirit of vengeance. As the Exodus story spoke to the Israelites in Babylonian exile, so "Creeping Death" spoke to alienated teenagers lost in high school hell, dreaming of the day they would be free.

Metallica's critique of organized religion is subtle. By simply telling part of the story of Exodus in "Creeping Death" Hetfield's lyrics expose the absurdity of belief in such a God. Likewise, as we shall see, by depicting televangelists and their victims in "Leper Messiah" Hetfield's lyrics comment on the sad state of Christianity in contemporary America. Follow the money and you will find corruption.

The album *Master of Puppets* is pure in the band's attempt to make music on their own terms. As the song "Damage, Inc."

declares and promises, the band are "Following our instinct not a trend / Go against the grain until the end." Among other things, Metallica refused to make a music video despite being courted by MTV. Their suspicion of money-chasers would continue, and only intensify, on the subsequent album . . . *And Justice for All*. For "One," a song on that album, Metallica would make their first video, but they did it on their own terms, choosing a seven-minute epic and filming in black and white. Metallica had no problem with making money as long as they were true to their art and not pandering to the public. This, of course, made the commercial sound of the next album, *Metallica* (a.k.a. The Black Album), all the more upsetting for some die-hard fans. But that is another story.

Recorded in 1985 and released in early 1986, *Master of Puppets* was a beacon of integrity shining on a crass American landscape. "Leper Messiah" saw and said what many knew in their hearts and minds: TV religion was the epitome of hypocritical nonsense. Even before Jim Bakker, Jimmy Swaggart, and others publicly fell from grace, Metallica pointed the finger at their ilk and at the people who followed them. Mocking the point of view of the greedy preacher, the song's chorus implores, "Send me money, send me green / Heaven you will meet / Make a contribution / And you'll get the better seat." The mix of money and salvation was nothing new. In fact, it led to the Protestant Reformation in 1517, when Martin Luther nailed his 95 theses to the door of All Saints' Church in Wittenberg to complain about the sale of indulgences, among other things.

The Roman Catholic Church, in which Luther served as a priest, sold indulgences that offered forgiveness for sins. A person could literally buy his way out of purgatory and into heaven. For those with money, buying indulgences was a lot easier than living in accord with Christian doctrine. Most of the money went straight to Rome, where it financed the lavish lifestyle of the popes and their grand building campaigns. Ironically, in 1980s America, it was Protestants, not Catholics, who were most associated with pay-to-play salvation. The promise that "you'll get the better seat" could refer to preferential treatment, including literally sitting up front in houses of worship. Metaphorically it is a promise of making it into heaven. Like the medieval popes, the modern televangelists embarked on building campaigns, erecting elaborate houses of worship. In addition, they enjoyed lavish lifestyles, with fine clothes and beautiful personal residences. Again, as in days gone by, most of the people footing the bill would never see the spectacles firsthand. But whereas most Catholics in the 1500s could only hear stories of the splendors in Rome, modern Americans could see pictures and even watch on TV.

The victims are not without blame for their gullibility, both with the indulgences and with the modern pleas to "send me money, send me green" with the promise that "heaven you will meet." The chorus concludes with the command to "bow to Leper Messiah." The enigmatic description raises questions. Why should we bow? And what is a leper messiah? The term is not in common use, even though the constituent words are plain enough.

A leper is someone who suffers from an infectious, fatal disease that manifests with disfigured skin. Leprosy has been nearly eradicated today, but in ancient times those who suffered from the disease were commonly banished from society to live among other lepers. Because disease was commonly thought to be divine punishment, there was little sympathy for lepers. These days we often use the term less literally and more metaphorically to describe social outcasts. If someone has done something terrible, they may be shunned like a leper.

A messiah is a savior for a group. Christians regard Jesus as *the* messiah. Jews do not recognize Jesus as messiah, but they do have a long tradition of waiting for a messiah.

Metallica got the phrase "leper messiah" from David Bowie, who uses it in the song "Ziggy Stardust." Kirk Hammett and Cliff Burton were both big Bowie fans and listened to the Ziggy Stardust album frequently on the Ride the Lightning Tour. It seems likely that Hammett or Burton suggested the phrase, or perhaps the phrase just stuck with Hetfield after hearing Hammett and Burton play the song. Bowie sings, "Making love with his ego / Ziggy sucked up into his mind, ah / Like a leper messiah / When the kids had killed the man / I had to break up the band." The song is part of the album *The Rise and Fall of Ziggy Stardust and the Spiders from Mars*, which tells the story of an androgynous rock star who conveys messages from extraterrestrial beings. In comparing Ziggy to a leper messiah, Bowie seems to be making him a kind of flawed Christ figure, which fits Ziggy's status as a murdered prophet. In the New Testament stories, Jesus miraculously healed lepers, connecting him with Moses (the deliverer) who was able to stick his hand inside his coat and pull it out full of leprosy, only to return it inside his coat and bring it back out fully healed. (It was a neat trick, but it didn't convince the pharaoh to free the Israelites.) Jesus, of course, made a habit of associating with not only lepers but also the dregs of society, including prostitutes, and other despised groups, such as tax collectors. Jesus was not a military messiah, but a savior of souls. Perhaps, at least in his own grandiose mind, Ziggy was also a man of the people, saving them with an extraterrestrial message.

Though "leper messiah" could be an apt description for Jesus, Bowie appears to be the first to use the phrase for its Christian imagery. Ironically, something close to the phrase "leper messiah" is found in the collection of Jewish texts known as the Talmud, which includes a story about how the Messiah would be found caring for lepers: "His name is 'the leper scholar,' as it is written, Surely he hath borne our griefs, and carried our sorrows: yet we did esteem him a leper, smitten of God, and afflicted. . . . 'When will the Messiah come?'—'Go and ask him himself,' was his reply. 'Where is he sitting?'—'At the entrance.' And by what sign may I recognize him?'—'He is sitting among the poor lepers . . .'" says the Talmud (Sanhedrin 98a and 98b). It is unlikely that Bowie had knowledge of the Talmud. So the best explanation is that he coined the phrase himself even though it wasn't completely original.

The question remains, however, what does "Leper Messiah" mean for the Metallica song? Hammett and Burton may have been inspired by Bowie to suggest the phrase, but the connection does not seem to go much beyond that. The figure of the Leper Messiah is richly ambiguous in the Metallica song. On the one hand, the reference to Jesus is clear, but on the other hand, the reference to a kind of false prophet or false messiah in the form of a fundamentalist preacher is also clear. Adding to the points of reference, the song also addresses "you"—the person who falls for the preacher's message. So we may also understand the title phrase as meaning a messiah for lepers, with "you" being a leper in the modern sense, a stigmatized person. Perhaps the preacher's message appeals particularly to the downtrodden masses who seek hope in his words.

Hetfield's lyrics begin, "Spineless from the start." Ironically, the song starts with aggressive instrumentation, with plenty of backbone. The first line continues, "Sucked into the part." Here we may have an allusion to Bowie's song with its line "Ziggy sucked up into his mind." For the moment "Leper Messiah" seems to be pointing the finger at the false prophet, who, like Ziggy, has a big ego that leads him into playing a grandiose role. The opening verse continues, "Circus comes to town, you play the lead clown." The circus is a form of distraction, pure entertainment with no redeeming value. The song's implication is that the televised megachurch spectacle is nothing but a circus. Beholding the sight, the false messiah is not appalled. Rather he sees a starring opportunity and gets the part of the lead clown, the preacher.

If we continue to interpret the verse as describing the preacher, then the next line takes aim at the story of Jesus. "Please, please / Spreading his disease, living by his story." The idea that religion is a disease or a virus implies that it is contagious, communicated from one person to another. (The lyric is likely also an allusion to the Anthrax album *Spreading the Disease*.) The result of religious belief is that one is compelled to give up one's own inclinations and preferences to live by someone else's story, to please the deity. The story of Jesus instructs us to give up worldly pursuits, live for others, and prepare for the kingdom to come. There is not much worldly power to be had in living that way. If you can convince others to live that way, however, you can exercise plenty of power over them and make lots of money. This is the move made by the preacher. The verse continues, "Knees, knees / Falling to your knees, suffer for his glory." Because the preacher's devotion is insincere, he will not be suffering for the glory of Jesus. So who will? The verse concludes with an answer, "You will." It is "you" who chose to follow the Leper Messiah, and "you" will suffer for the Leper Messiah's glory—not the glory of Jesus.

This twist to a second-person address at the end of the verse prompts us to look back to the beginning of the verse. The ambiguity encourages us to interpret certain lines as applying to both the Leper Messiah and those who follow him. Now we can hear "spineless from the start" as describing the followers, who do not have the backbone or the intellectual courage to think for themselves and so are "sucked into the part" of "lead clown." They are suckers who end up playing the role of the fool. In this line of interpretation, the followers are the ones who spread the disease of the false preacher and live by his story, the story the preacher tells rather than the genuine teaching of Jesus.

We are now in a position to make sense of the first lines of the chorus, "Time for lust, time for lie / Time to kiss your life goodbye." For "you" life as you knew it is over. You're not in charge anymore. Pascal's Wager famously recommended that we should bet on belief in God because we have everything to gain and nothing to lose. Metallica's song makes an important correction to Pascal's Wager. In fact, we have a lot to lose if we follow a false prophet and believe in a God that doesn't exist. We lose the chance to live our worldly life the way we would want to, and we get nothing in return. No more lusting and lying for you! You are stuck living a life in which the most important thing is to keep your soul pure and worthy of heaven. To the extent that you fall short, you are filled with anxiety and guilt. On the other hand, for the preacher it is precisely time to lust and lie. The illusion is maintained through lies and deceit. The chorus depicts the preacher imploring, "Send me money, send me green." With money comes power and worldly temptation. Leper Messiahs like Jim Bakker and Jimmy Swaggart were known for their lavish lifestyles, and eventually they were undone when their sexual improprieties became public. Here

Hetfield acts as prophet, not only condemning the sins of the age but forecasting the demise of the hypocritical sinners in the pulpits. It is tempting to condemn such Leper Messiahs as con artists, but the truth is likely more complicated than that. Men like Bakker and Swaggart probably began with sincere religious belief and were corrupted by success and power. In their own minds they probably justified their deceit and greed in terms of the good they were doing in spreading the gospel message and providing religious comfort to the masses.

The verse after the chorus holds the masses responsible for wanting religious comfort so badly that they fall for the con game. "Marvel at his tricks, need your Sunday fix." The tricks of the televangelist might include healing. Often this was a setup in which someone with no actual ailment faked spontaneous recovery. Short of that chicanery, there was the promise of answered prayers. "Send me money, send me green," and your prayers will be answered. On a less miraculous level was simply the promise that God loves and cares for you, as long as you worship him and send me money.

Rather than feel sorry for the people who fall for this deception, the narrator wags a finger at them by comparing them to drug addicts: "Need your Sunday fix." For the person hooked on heroin, the drug ceases to be an occasional indulgence and a source of euphoria. Instead, it becomes a necessity. If the addict is without the drug for too long, he will start to go into withdrawal. At that point, he feels broken and needs a fix. The heroin just gets him to feeling normal again, and in the grips of the addiction a person ceases to care what humiliating or immoral actions he has to take to get that fix.

This comparison between drugs and religion is not original. Karl Marx famously called religion the opiate of the masses. As

Marx saw it, religion brought people comfort, promising them that there was a God who loved them and a better world to come in the next life. It's less well known, but Marx also called religion "the heart of a heartless world." He did not blame the masses who took refuge in religion. Rather he hoped and planned for a supposedly better world in which the opiate comforts of religion would no longer be necessary and religion would disappear. The narrator of "Leper Messiah" has no such sympathy and no hopes or grand plans for the future. Instead, he tries to shake people out of their false comfort so that they can make the most of life, even in a heartless world.

The verse continues with more finger wagging: "Blind devotion came, Rotting your brain." *You* fell for the con. *You* swallowed it hook, line, and sinker. The result is "blind devotion." Looking outside yourself to those who know better is fine, but authorities, religious or otherwise, must be challenged and examined. Consider Dostoevsky's sinister character the Grand Inquisitor. He is a kind of Leper Messiah who insists that people want to hand over their freedom and be told what to believe: "I tell thee that man is tormented by no greater anxiety than to find someone quickly to whom he can hand over that gift of freedom." The Grand Inquisitor describes blind devotion, and we can understand its appeal in a heartless world in which so few choices seem available—and a world in which the choices that we do have cause terrible anxiety. The feeling of certainty that comes with blind devotion relieves us of that anxiety and replaces it with a sense of superiority over those who lack it, those who lack faith. However, when we give up the right to think for ourselves, our mental muscles atrophy and our brains rot. If we are lucky, the Leper Messiah will simply drain our bank accounts, but it could get worse. As Voltaire observed, "Those who can make you believe absurdities, can make you commit atrocities." Religious wars and violence sometimes result. Thankfully, aggression is not part of the narrative of "Leper Messiah." Instead, *you* with your rotting brain are simply condemned to mental imprisonment and to "join the endless chain" of mindless followers. You give up your freedom to define yourself and to live life on your own terms. As a result, you become one of the homogenized many who follow the great leader, the Leper Messiah.

The need for comfort and relief from anxiety is clear, but the appeal of the Leper Messiah goes beyond that. You are "taken by his glamour." Lots of religious leaders are promising salvation in the world to come, but the Leper Messiah is enjoying worldly success. He is rich and famous, living his life on television. The Lord seems to have favored him and blessed him with golden charisma and a silver tongue. By following the Leper Messiah you partake in his glory and maybe, just maybe, some of it will rub off on you. If you pray the right way and send enough money, worldly wealth may somehow be yours. That is the implicit, and often explicit, message of the Leper Messiah's gospel of prosperity. By contrast, the poverty and suffering of Jesus, never mind caring for the sick (like actual lepers), is unappealing. The Leper Messiah seems to have a direct line to Jesus, and he tells you that Jesus wants you to prosper and have it all.

Perhaps even more than money, the Leper Messiah craves "fame, fame." His ego bloats with adoration. But how to get more? The song answers, "Infection is the game." The Leper Messiah seeks to infect his followers who will infect others in turn. He can't do it all himself. The song's first verse depicts him as "spreading his disease." It is not, however, a disease that he himself has. The preacher's belief is largely false and cynical, not genuine. He counts on others being taken by his glamour and charisma to the point where they cease thinking for themselves. Their brains rot and become susceptible to infection. The followers find comfort and relief from anxiety, and other people are attracted and imitate them, leading to further infection. The Leper Messiah beholds the result with pleasure and satisfaction. He now has what he wanted even more than money and fame. He is "stinking drunk with power." In his intoxication the Leper Messiah gets a thrill out of telling people what to do. They will listen to anything he says, not only how to pray and how much to pay, but what to wear and how to vote. The song paints a grim picture, but there is hope in the two words that close the verse: "We see." Although many of "you" have fallen for the Leper Messiah's deception, "we see" the truth. "We" speaks for the point of view of the narrator and others who have retained an independent perspective. Alas, there is no rescue for "you."

After a return to the chorus, the final verse forecasts doom for "you." Hetfield barks the first line, "Witchery, weakening." It is as if the preacher has cast a spell on "you." How else can "we" explain the transformation you have undergone? The work of the witchery is "weakening." Previously, a disease has been described as rotting your brain. Less physical and more meta-physical, the occult description of witchery suggests that your free will has been diminished. Not only do you no longer think for yourself, but you can no longer act for yourself. You simply act as one among many. The preacher speaks, and you, in chorus with everyone else, say amen. The preacher asks, *Will you obey?* Along with everyone else you say, *I will.* The "I" is an illusion though. "You" have lost your sense of self.

Drunk with power, the Leper Messiah "sees the sheep are gathering." In the Gospel of John (10:11–18) Jesus describes himself as the Good Shepherd, who is willing to lay down his life to keep the sheep safe. And in the Gospel of Matthew (25:31–46), Jesus says that when the Son of Man separates the sheep from the goats, the sheep will inherit the kingdom. The sheep are those who have cared for one another when they were sick, hungry, or lonely and in doing so loved the Lord. According to this imagery, the sheep represent the good, and the goats represent the wicked who care only for themselves with their lust and their lies. In the song, the Leper Messiah is not the good shepherd who loves and cares for his flock, and the sheep are not going to inherit the kingdom. Rather, the sheep are people who have acted like mindless herd animals, following a cynical leader who seeks to use them for his own power and glory. The Leper Messiah is certainly not willing to lay down his life for his flock. Quite the contrary, he requires that they give up their lives, or at least their freedom for him. This again calls to mind Dostoevsky's Grand Inquisitor, who praises his own success in subordinating his followers, saying, "Men rejoiced that they were again led like sheep and that the terrible gift that had brought them such suffering was lifted from their hearts." The "terrible gift" that had been taken from them was their freedom. The suggestion is that freedom is a curse and a burden; freedom makes human life harder. People are basically sheep, and they are happier when they live like sheep, going with the crowd, directed by a leader. So, in essence, the Leper Messiah is just giving people what they want, a set of orders to follow unquestioningly. Sadly, though, the sheep will ultimately find themselves on his table.

The verse continues, "Set the trap, hypnotize." The promises of heaven have been a lie. Worse, they have been a trap. Your brain has rotted, your free will has been lost. Moving from the occult witchery at the beginning of the verse, the conclusion depicts the final trap as hypnosis, a fitting description of how the insane behavior is induced. Along these lines, the philosopher Friedrich Nietzsche says that madness is rare in individuals, but in crowds it is the rule. People lose their sense of identity and individuality in a crowd and become willing to do things they otherwise would not do. We see some of this when behavior goes bad at a sporting event or concert, but we also see it in religious gatherings and political rallies. Think of the hypnotic power Hitler had over audiences. Thankfully, the Leper Messiah is not calling for violence against some other group. Instead he is calling for extreme self-sacrifice to support his mission, his church, his glory. "Send me money, send me green." Don't worry if you can't afford it. Give until it hurts, and then keep giving some more. The verse concludes, "Now you follow." Driven by the speed of the music, we can easily imagine the followers as lemmings rushing over a cliff to their own demise.

The song returns to the verse telling "you" to kiss your life goodbye and issuing its false promise that "heaven you will meet." Then, resuming the perspective of the narrator, the song concludes with the chant of "Lie, lie, lie . . ." We thus have a cautionary tale of sheep who sacrifice themselves for a heavenly reward they will never receive. Any genuine Christian can endorse the song's warning that there are false preachers who will bleed you dry if you let them. Not everyone who speaks in the name of Christ is a true witness. However, the song also speaks to people who find Christianity as a whole to be nothing but a con, a false promise. To the extent that Christianity asks you to sacrifice worldly happiness for the questionable promise of a better life in heaven, it is a slave morality, a philosophy fit for sheep. We need to keep looking if we are to find something of value in the message of Jesus. One place, for sure, that we won't find it is in the promise to work magic and produce healing miracles.

The line "Now you *follow*" links *Master of Puppets* to The Black Album, where you "*follow* the god that failed." Here it is not a charismatic Leper Messiah who seduces you, but a magical creed. *The God That Failed* was the title of a book published in 1949, which collected accounts of people who had turned away from communism. In the song "The God That Failed" Hetfield offers his testimony as someone who was raised as a Christian Scientist and who turned away from that denomination. The song does not specifically invoke the Christian Scientist creed, but it is consistent with it, and it seems partly inspired by Hetfield's mother's refusal of treatment for cancer. More broadly, then, the song serves as a critique of forms of Christianity that rely on "miracle, mystery, and authority," as the Grand Inquisitor might say. The question left unanswered by the song is whether there are forms of Christianity that are immune to Hetfield's critique.

"The God That Failed" begins with a takedown of hypocritical false humility. "Pride you took / Pride you feel / Pride that you felt when you'd kneel." In a parable (Luke 18:9-14), Jesus criticized a Pharisee who made a great show of praying in public, wanting to be seen and thought holy. Clearly this man was guilty of the sin of pride. But prayer doesn't need to be public to be prideful. You don't need to be preaching on a street corner or taking a place of prominence in a church or synagogue. Getting on your knees, even in the privacy of your own home, can be filled with a sense of spiritual superiority, as perhaps it was for Hetfield's parents. There is nothing necessarily wrong with prayer on one's knees, just as there is nothing necessarily wrong with prayer in public. Rather, it is the spirit in which the prayer is said that matters. Whatever the proper spirit may be, it is not pride.

In the second verse, the song suggests that pride has misdirected prayer. "Not the word / Not the love / Not what you thought from above." The Gospel of John (1:1) famously declares, "In the beginning was the Word, and the Word was with God, and the Word was God." "The Word" refers to Jesus as co-eternal and one with God the Father. So the song's suggestion is that what "you" are praying to is not Jesus, not God. The song's target, "you," may refer to Hetfield's parents and other Christian Scientists, but "you" refers more broadly to anyone subscribing to a certain kind of false religion. In truth, Jesus is associated with a message of love, a command to love one another and to love even one's enemies. The song, though, clearly says that whatever your prayer is directed at, it is "not the love." As the song will reveal, your prayer is directed at some source of magical healing power instead. The final line of the verse, "Not what you thought from above," is unclear, but the past tense may suggest that there was a time when you thought differently about what was above. This interpretation is supported by the next verse, in which "It feeds / It grows / It clouds all that you will know." The imagery suggests that something gradually takes over and dominates your way of thinking. The takeover does not happen all at once. It is not a charismatic preacher who hypnotizes you and takes your money. Instead, it is a magical creed about Jesus, who supposedly healed lepers, and who will work similar miracles for you if you have faith.

The verse depicts the magical creed as a parasite that feeds off you, its host. The indefinite designation "It" strikes a creepy chord. Like an unseen tapeworm, "It" sparks morbid imagination. The parasitic system of belief feeds off you and grows. A creed cannot survive without a host. "Leper Messiah" plays with a different medical analogy, likening the dissemination of dogma to the spread of a contagious disease. In "The God That Failed" the emphasis is on the damage done to the individual and those closely connected. The irony of the situation is that "It" can only survive if it keeps you alive, and yet what it demands may kill you.

Metallica's next studio album, *Load*, featured "Until It Sleeps," a song inspired by Hetfield's father's suffering and death from cancer in 1996, shortly after they had partially reconciled. "It" is a potent designation for cancer inasmuch as it feeds and grows within a person, and if it is not eliminated it will kill the person, the host on which it feeds. When the verse concludes that "It clouds all that you will know" we can picture the religious creed as brain cancer that has altered its host's way of thinking. "You" can no longer think clearly; everything is seen through the obscuring lens of religion.

The impersonal nature of "It" makes blame difficult. People get mad at cancer, but cancer does not have a mind of its own and thus has no evil intent. By contrast, we can readily point the finger at the Leper Messiah, who casts his spell and hypnotizes the flock for his gain at their expense. So we might think that there is no real blame to assign in "The God That Failed." That is not so, however. The next verse has an accusatory tone: "Deceit / Deceive / Decide just what you believe." If there is deceit, there must be a deceiver. Who is it? "Dyers Eve" from . . . *And Justice for All* seems to answer plainly: "Dear Mother / Dear Father / What is this hell you have put me through / Believer / Deceiver." The curious thing about the accusation is that Hetfield labels his parents as both believers *and* deceivers. If they really believed that modern medicine wasn't necessary because Jesus would heal the faithful, then in what sense is it fair to call them deceivers?

A deceiver is purposely lying, not just spreading a false belief. The fact is that Hetfield's parents were deceived by someone else, who in turn was deceived by someone else. How does the deception get started? Is there a cynical liar at the start? Not necessarily.

Belief in healing without medicine may be sincere to start, and it may be able to point to some success. After all, some illnesses get better on their own over time; occasionally even cancer goes into remission in ways that defy medical explanation. Magical belief should cease, though, when the evidence mounts that prayer will not bring the desired results the way that medical care will. A community of believers who have become an institution may resist such evidence, however, by blaming the victim. For example, it may be said that the person's prayers were not sincere enough, or they did not believe strongly enough, or they had some secret sin. If blaming the victim won't work in a particular case, the community of believers can simply tell themselves that God works in mysterious ways. We never know what greater purpose or plan God has in mind whereby he will bring good out of what appears, for the moment, to be a bad outcome. In this way, independent thought is discouraged. You, as a mere mortal, cannot see the big picture that God has in mind. So, instead of trying to make sense of the situation, you should have faith in God and trust the collective wisdom of your religious community, which will "decide just what you believe." This is a big pill to swallow, though.

In order to be this kind of believer, you must also be a deceiver, a self-deceiver. The song continues, "I see faith in your eyes / Never you hear the discouraging lies." The narrator speaks from the point of view of one who has rejected the god that failed, and he addresses the believer. The believer's eyes express faith, a commitment to believe despite the discouraging sights those eyes may have witnessed: such as a child whose broken arm heals badly when treated with prayer. The believer must be a self-deceiver by not acknowledging what he clearly sees, and also by not scrutinizing the faulty explanations he hears. The lies that explain the healing failures should be discouraging, and on a certain level they are.

Self-deception is puzzling. We all know it occurs, and we are all guilty of it to one degree or another. Yet how can it possibly work? How can you lie to yourself? If you know the truth, then how can you lie to yourself successfully? It's like playing hide-and-go-seek with yourself—it shouldn't work. Thankfully we don't have to solve that philosophical and psychological puzzle here except to say that human beings are complicated and good at focusing on what they want to believe even when some other part of them is telling them that it isn't true.

The conflicted nature of self-deception is captured in the song's next line, "I hear faith in your cries." The believer, "you," cries in response to the lack of healing, expressing sorrow but also expressing faith. There is no faith without doubt, and what "you" see causes doubt that you struggle to overcome with belief. Again and again "you" are confronted with the truth that prayer won't work as well as medicine, and the struggle to overcome doubt gets harder and more painful. The institution, the community of believers, and your loved ones have all told you something that is not true, and on some level you feel dispirited and disappointed. As the song says, "Broken is the promise, betrayal." You thought you had a deal, an agreement that if you believed and prayed in a certain way, then healing would result. If that was the promise, it has been broken repeatedly. Yes, explanations have been offered, but you cannot help feeling betrayed. Judas notoriously betrayed Jesus, and so the word has real resonance. Betrayal is a damning sin.

Blasphemously and poetically, the verse continues with a description of the crucified Jesus: "The healing hand held back by the deepened nail." At first it may seem that Jesus betrayed you, but a moment's reflection reveals that it is your fellow believers who have deceived you and encouraged you to deceive yourself. That is the real betrayal. Rather than teach you to examine reality critically, they have taught you to hide from it. They have promised truth and delivered lies. How could a man who was crucified over 2,000 years ago heal you today? The hand that is supposed to heal was nailed to a cross. (Actually, most scholars believe the nails would have gone through the wrists to better support the body.) If prayer actually delivered healing, then that would be miraculous evidence, but when prayer does not deliver, you are left to "follow the god that failed."

Having invested personal pride (not to mention time and money), plenty of people will continue to follow this failed god. In fact, some religious believers interpret contrary evidence as a challenge to test their faith. Thus it becomes a badge of spiritual pride to believe in the face of evidence and to twist logic and reason to make failure look like success. This is the kind of pride that is mocked in the first verse.

In between disappointments the believer returns to a state of normalcy where the terrible doubts are silenced by dubious explanations and reaffirmations of faith. The song continues with a description of the rebuilding work of self-deception: "Find your peace / Find your say / Find the smooth road on your way." In the face of God's failure to deliver what you think has been promised, you must make sense of the situation. Rationalization aids self-deception, providing reasons you can only half-believe.

But with time and effort, you focus only on those reasons, turning a blind eye and a deaf ear to the nagging evidence to the contrary. As a result, you "find your peace." More than that, you "find your say." Not only do you have a way of reconciling things in your own mind, but you once again become a vocal proponent for this apparently failed God. You testify to others that they must have faith and not believe the evidence of their eyes. Faith is a struggle, yes. However, you grow stronger, more muscular, in your faith through the struggle, and you move forward to "find the smooth road on your way."

With its next verse, though, the song undercuts and mocks the possibility of moving forward. "Trust you gave / A child to save / Left you cold and him in grave." This is no mere failure to heal a broken arm or relieve a fever. The description comes in the past tense and functions as a surprise revelation in the storytelling of the song. The death of one's child is not the kind of thing that should be easily overcome with a bit of rationalization that sets you back on your smooth road of faith. Notice that "you" gave the trust. The child was too young to know whether or not to trust prayer to heal him. So the child simply trusted you, and you put your trust in the healing power of God. Hopefully, that trust did not come easily to you. Hopefully, you struggled, thinking that it would be one thing to risk your own life this way but that it is another to risk your child's life. Perhaps you consulted with community members. They reassured you that they understood your doubts and hesitation, but that you must put your trust in God. Of course, that was easy for them to say, since it wasn't their child at risk. Hopefully, that is how it happened. Alternatively, maybe you consulted no one but God. Maybe your pride kept you from voicing your doubts to other people. So, as the first verse depicts, you took pride even when you kneeled.

Whichever way the scenario unfolded, we know the result. The child died. You were shocked, left cold. This could have, perhaps should have, moved you to reconsider your faith in this God. But who left you cold? God? Or the people who told you to put your trust in the healing power of Jesus?

In a previous verse, the narrator describes the "healing hand" of Jesus as "held back by the deepened nail." You did not heed that warning when the stakes were lower, a broken arm or a fever, and now, thanks to a more serious illness, the result is "him in grave." The child is dead and buried. This obvious interpretation of the lyric certainly fits, but the ambiguity of "him," coupled with the earlier description of "the healing hand held back by the deepened nail," invites another interpretation. Not only is the child dead and buried, but so is Jesus. Perhaps he was just a man, a gifted spiritual teacher who is mistakenly worshipped as a God. Clearly, the God of the Christian Scientists, who is called on to heal the sick without medicine, has failed. That does not mean, however, that there are no more members of the Christian Scientist faith. Indeed, it continues to this day. Remember that the song's title is taken from a 1949 book written by people who abandoned communism. Communism has largely been discredited, but like the Christian Scientist faith, it is still around.

Metallica's song does not necessarily apply beyond Christian Scientists to adherents of Christianity more generally. Despite the prevalence of Leper Messiahs in the form of predatory preachers, maybe Christianity delivers truth. Over a century before The Black Album, Nietzsche declared that God is dead. What he meant was that belief in the God of the Judeo-Christian tradition had become worn-out, tired, obsolete. Science had stepped in to provide explanations for the things that used to require God. In the modern scientific age, it had become unreasonable to believe in a God who long ago intervened in human affairs to perform saving miracles. With no miracles occurring these days and with science explaining the workings of the natural world, God was as dead as disco. Notice, that doesn't mean that no one believes in God anymore. People were saying "disco is dead" when disco records were still on the charts, and disco remains today in some form, even if only for nostalgia. So Nietzsche wasn't saying that belief in God had disappeared, nor that it would disappear completely anytime soon.

The ambiguities in Hetfield's lyrics leave it an open question as to whether he would have agreed not only that the God of the Christian Scientists had failed, but also that the God of the Judeo-Christian tradition had failed and was dead. Even if one does not think that God is dead, one must admit that he is hidden. The great medieval theologian and philosopher Thomas Aquinas spoke of "deus absconditus"—the absconded God, the hidden God. God may have made his presence clear in earlier times, but for now he has withdrawn from view, no longer working clear and obvious miracles, no longer making appearances. Why would God do this? No one knows. One explanation is that God's hiddenness makes a greater place for faith. According to this explanation, if God made his presence obvious, we would be overwhelmed, and our free will would be compromised. Maybe. But that doesn't explain why God's appearance to people in the past didn't compromise their free will.

Whatever Hetfield's earlier views on Christianity in general may have been, they likely have changed. In the process of his recovery from alcoholism, as documented in the film *Metallica: Some Kind of Monster* up until the time of his relapse in 2019, Hetfield seems to have embraced a higher power. Indeed, some of his tattoos, including the cross on his chest, seem to suggest

**THE MEANING OF METALLICA**

that he has accepted some form of Christianity. There is nothing necessarily hypocritical about this. Hetfield is intensely private, and for all we know he may always have accepted some form of Christianity. On the other hand, like many other people who have dealt with alcoholism and other addictions, he may have found that belief in a higher power was a key element of his recovery. To be clear, not everyone who successfully recovers from addiction believes in God. It is perfectly possible to be an agnostic or atheist and successfully work a program of recovery—it's just not easy. So the legitimate concern that could be raised about Hetfield is that he took the easy way, believing in God, out of desperation. According to the old saying, there are no atheists in foxholes. Of course, this is not strictly correct, but it does contain important insight, namely, desperate circumstances often lead to desperate actions. For all we know, Hetfield came to believe in God over the course of time, or perhaps he believed all along. If the desperation of finding himself in the foxhole of alcoholism motivated him to believe, we should walk a mile in his shoes and be careful in rendering any judgment of him. Indeed, we are all "On a quest, meaning, reason . . . Twisting / Turning / Through the never."

# CHAPTER 2

# ADDICTION

*When Sweet Amber Becomes
the Master of Puppets*

The issue that connects Hetfield's lyrics on religion to his lyrics on addiction is self-deception. Whether or not he is presently guilty of self-deception with regard to religious belief, he has certainly pointed the finger at others in the past. When it comes to addiction, early on, Hetfield displayed a keen eye and a sharp tongue in describing the self-deceptive plight of the addict. Indeed, the title track from *Master of Puppets* offers an unsparing appraisal of the addict's condition, as he spirals out of control in a race towards death.

Certainly, the song may be interpreted more broadly to apply to multiple situations in which a person has unwittingly become a pawn in a game, making moves against his own self-interest. In fact, this theme plays out across several songs on the album, including "Disposable Heroes," in which the "soldier boy" is manipulated to sacrifice his life for a cause he does not understand or believe in, and "Leper Messiah," in which the sheep follow the shepherd right to the slaughter.

The title track's refrain is chilling, with the puppet master personified and speaking, indeed boasting: "Master of puppets I'm pulling your strings / Twisting your mind and smashing your dreams / Blinded by me, you can't see a thing / Just call my name, 'cause I'll hear you scream." These lines on their own could easily apply to many scenarios. We could imagine these words issuing from the Leper Messiah, who gleefully celebrates the mindless dependence he has created in his flock. Or we could imagine them spoken by the military commander in "Disposable Heroes," who likewise takes sinister pride in the way he has dissolved the independence of his "soldier boy." In fact, the commander mocks the soldier boy with the instruction, "Back to the front / You coward / You servant / You blind man." As in the title track, the victim is described as servile and slavish. Appropriately, the album cover for *Master of Puppets* depicts the outcome of "Disposable Heroes," with the crosses in the military graveyard connected to puppet strings and sinister hands in the sky. The key line in the title track's refrain is "Blinded by me, you can't see a thing." This applies across songs and scenarios. Whether it is a preacher, a general, or a drug, you can't see the puppet strings, at least not at first.

The audience for a puppet show cannot see the thin strings from a distance, but up close they become clear. So how can anyone enjoy a puppet show when they can see the strings? The answer is willing suspension of disbelief. When watching an artistic performance, we put aside, or suspend, our disbelief in impossible occurrences. Likewise, we willingly forget for the moment that the characters are not real. We do all this for the sake of enjoying the fiction; we ignore the puppet strings. There is no harm in cooperating with such entertainment, and in fact entering the world of fictions can help us make sense of similar circumstances in the real world. The harm comes when we do not readjust to reality. The person who, for example, spends nearly all his waking hours inhabiting a different personality and profile in a video game has a problem.

As we've seen before, successful deception routinely requires our cooperation in the form of self-deception. In "The God That Failed," for example, others may be deceiving you about the healing power of God, but the deception will not work fully, or forever, if you don't play along. Nonetheless, in the religious example there is still someone outside yourself to share the blame. By contrast, the truly horrific situation for the addict is that there is no person outside oneself to blame. The puppet master is not a person, but a drug, or rather your own addiction to the drug. Worse, no one but yourself makes you take that drug. So when the master of puppets speaks in the song, it is not even the drug speaking. The illicit substance sitting in a bag never hurt anyone, and some people can indulge without becoming addicted. The master is your own self-destructive desire for the drug.

You think you are the master, using the drug to elevate your mood and enhance your performance. You come to think that you do everything better with the help of the drug. The drug is your servant, your slave, your tool. You think you use it, but your desire ends up using you, like a parasite. You think you are the master, but as the title track repeats, "Blinded by me, you can't see a thing."

How can you be so blind? Well, at first the drug really does have a lot to offer. It makes you feel great, and lots of good times roll when you're high. The negatives are easy to ignore at first: the cost in cash, the embarrassing mishaps, the comedown, and the need for more. With time, though, life becomes organized around the drug, and your priorities shift. Still, you barely notice that the drug use is "twisting your mind and smashing your dreams." This is a theme that Hetfield revisited in later songs, for example "The End of the Line" from *Death Magnetic*, in which the reversal of power is explicit: "The slave becomes the master / Need more and more / Right now and ever after." The need for more is met, of course, by the master's promise: "Just call my name, 'cause I'll hear you scream." In "Dirty Window" from *St. Anger*, Hetfield laments, "I drink from the cup of denial." Fittingly, denial is a key element in the self-deception that enables addiction. The insistence that *I don't have a problem* and that *I have it under control* is maintained only by turning a blind eye to the facts and denying what is obvious from the outside and should be obvious to you.

Ironically, Hetfield wrote "Master of Puppets" when he was a full-blown alcoholic. It would be another 15 years or so until he fully admitted his problem and got sober, but at the time he was in the grip of an addiction no less serious than the drug addiction he was writing about. "Motorbreath" from the debut album, *Kill 'Em All*, refers not just to life in the fast lane and the speed of the music but to the bad breath of speed users, with a tacit acknowledgment that the band had indulged in the drug at the time. There is no clear indication, though, that Hetfield had problems with drugs. Early in their career, Metallica were affectionately known as "Alcoholica." Rather than shy away from the moniker, the band embraced it and promoted their image as rowdy guys who liked to get shitfaced and cause a little senseless destruction. If Hetfield thought of himself as an alcoholic at this stage, it was not with any serious self-censure. He may have needed alcohol, but he thought of himself as getting the better of the bargain. He was, after all, at the peak of his creative power. Later songs, like "Sweet Amber," tell the story of denial and self-realization. For now, though, we return to the song that started it all.

The lyrics of "Master of Puppets" begin abruptly with "End of passion play." So, in a sense, we start at the end. A traditional passion play reenacts the suffering and abuse of Jesus, from his scourging through his suffering and death on the cross. Such a play does not include a scene of resurrection—the celebration of resurrection is left for Easter Sunday. If there is no resurrection, then the suffering of the passion is in vain. As we know, there is no comeback, no resurrection in the story told by "Master of Puppets." Indeed, the song ends with the promise of death, linking it to the album cover's graveyard.

The second part of the opening line describes "crumbling away." By "End of passion play" we've been told in effect that the story will end in death. The tormentors of Jesus were not subtle, and his wounds were not self-inflicted. By contrast, the song will tell the story of someone whose life crumbles away. He thinks he is on top of the world, but all the while he himself is chipping away at the structure of his life. The first explanation of the imminent demise comes in the next line, "I'm your source of self-destruction." So, from the start, it is clear that this is not a story of victimization but of self-sabotage. Eerily, the narrator speaks to himself, combining first-person speech and second-person address. Alas, the voice will not be recognized by the person, the puppet.

Conjuring drug imagery, the narrator describes "veins that pump with fear, sucking darkest clear." Death will not come quickly, easily, or passively. Rather, you will take an active role in "leading on your death's construction." Your demise will be built by your own self-deceptive actions. With open eyes, though, you need to take the first small action: "Taste me you will see." Of course, you will not literally be tasting, but rather snorting or smoking. The word fits, though, because a taste is tiny, just a sample. That is all it will take, however, before the addiction kicks in and "more is all you need." For the addict, there is no such thing as enough; there is only the desire for more and more. So, by the end of the first verse, "You're dedicated to / How I'm killing you."

The warning is simultaneously announced and ignored, because the self-destruction of addiction requires self-deception. It will drive you to your knees, and you won't even realize it. No, you will not be kneeling in prayer, but you may be crawling across a rug the morning after the party looking for cocaine caught in carpet fibers. You will still think you are on top of the world, but in reality, you "Come crawling faster / Obey your master." The desire for the drug whips up a frantic pace—as "your life burns faster" you "obey your master."

In case there is any doubt about who is in charge at this point, the song breaks into the refrain with which we began: "Master of puppets I'm pulling your strings / Twisting your mind and smashing your dreams / Blinded by me, you can't see a thing / Just call my name, 'cause I'll hear you scream." The imagery calls to mind Black Sabbath's "Snowblind," a song about cocaine addiction in which Ozzy Osbourne wails, "My eyes are blind but I can see." These lyrics provide a powerful combination of admission and denial—I'm blind (from the drug), but I can actually see better (from the drug). "Snowblind" culminates in an angry, defensive verse in which the narrator berates anyone who would try to tell him that he has a problem: "Don't you think I know what I'm doing / Don't tell me that it's doing me wrong / You're the one who's really the loser / This is where I feel I belong." Certainly, the same sentiments trap the puppet in Metallica's song.

For a time, even though the drug takes its toll, it continues to deliver its high, its promise. The next verse, though, focuses exclusively on the negative effects, beginning with the poetic phrase "needlework the way." For the addict, injecting the drug is a major step, one that most begin their drug use by saying they will never take. For a while, their way of assuring others that they don't have a problem is that they don't shoot up. In time, however, the needle promises the most effective delivery of the drug, the best high. So the addict makes himself look at the process differently. Shooting up is no longer a mark of shame, but a badge of honor. Indeed it becomes an artform. "Needlework" refers to decorative sewing and textile production. With this description, the act of tapping a vein is transformed into something akin to knitting, a soft decorative art. The addict's self-delusion is not so severe as to mistake track marks for mittens, but a new way of seeing has transformed the ugly into the beautiful.

The line that begins "Needlework the way" concludes "never you betray." The "you" is ambiguous. On the one hand, "you" seems to refer to the addict, the puppet. You have become a faithful follower of the drug; you are steadfast in your devotion. This is ironic in the sense that you have lost much of your power of choice, such that you are better described as dependent than faithful. On the other hand, "you" may refer to the drug, which never disappoints, never betrays. In a world that constantly disappoints us, the drug can be counted on to deliver. It is the friend or lover who will never be unfaithful. This is significant in light of the later song "The God That Failed" in which "broken is the promise, betrayal." As discussed in chapter 1, the word "betray" resonates with religious significance, calling to mind Judas turning traitor on Jesus. In "The God That Failed" belief in the healing power of Jesus does not deliver on its promise, and the result is the feeling of betrayal. If religion fails you, solace may be sought in drugs. For a time, the drugs console, but, as the verse goes on to detail, the drugs end up betraying the user. For a while, drugs both give and take, but in time the taking eclipses the giving.

The next line describes the state of play for the addict who is needleworking the way, "life of death becoming clearer." The casual listener may mis-hear the phrase as "life *or* death." That dichotomy would represent a stark choice and a crucial decision, but it would first require a realization. Because there is no such realization, there is no choice or decision confronting the puppet. Rather, he is living a life *of* death, a life that is not really a life in the fullest human sense, but a mere existence. Gone is any sense of love or connection to other people, replaced by slavish and selfish devotion to feeding his drug habit. Zombie-like, the addict dwells among the walking dead. The line concludes with the phrase "becoming clearer." We must wonder, though, to whom is it becoming clearer? Certainly not to the puppet. The insidious nature of the addiction trap is such that he does not realize he is trapped. He does not recognize or admit that his life has been hollowed out, that he is a shell of a man staggering in a state of living death. Instead, it is the outside observer to whom the life of death has become clearer. Not just any outside observer, however. Other addicts may see the puppet's life as normal, reinforcing each other in their acceptance of degradation. It is only to the person who is not an addict that the "life of death" is clear.

Despite being in a state of denial, the addict will hide his condition and will not admit the depth of his suffering. The "pain monopoly" is experienced from a first-person perspective; people who care for the puppet will not know or feel the pain directly. The phrase is ambiguous and evocative. Does the drug have a monopoly on the puppet's pain? Or does pain have a monopoly on the puppet's feelings? Perhaps both, perhaps neither. The drug has come to cause the puppet prodigious pain, no doubt. This is sad and ironic in that the drug was first taken to escape the pain of life, with its struggles, disappointments, and absurdities. For a while it worked. In time, though, it worked less and less as the puppet needed more and more, until it worked only a little and mostly just to relieve the pain of withdrawal and to satisfy the craving for what the puppet might wish he didn't want. The pain of the world has not disappeared. In fact, it has only gotten worse as the addict has become less capable of living a normal life and taking normal responsibilities. Bills remain unpaid, relationships are frayed, and the body aches. The only remedy for the pain caused by the drug is more of the drug—it is both disease and cure. So the drug may not have a complete monopoly on the puppet's pain, but it certainly has the largest share of the market.

Pain, though, has pretty close to a monopoly on the puppet's feelings. Gone are the good times, and fleeting are the moments of relief that the drug delivers. Emotional pain fills his existence of "ritual misery." At first, there was excitement in the whole process of buying the drug, using it, and partying through the night. The illegal enterprise can be a thrilling, adrenaline-inducing ride. There might even be something sacred or quasi-religious in the experience, the steps taken, the ritual involved, but in time, the experience fades from ritual ecstasy into ritual misery. There is no joy, only hassle involved in scoring and consuming the drug. You are stuck in a loop of using the drug, jonesing for more, and desperately seeking to satisfy your craving. If you're lucky, there's some cocaine left over from the night before and you "chop your breakfast on a mirror." There is nothing glamorous about it. You don't want the drug, you need it. As the master says, "You're dedicated to / How I'm killing you."

The master dances the puppet around, making him crawl and obey. In a moment of clarity, though, the puppet sees the strings, and the narration switches to his point of view. Fueled by anger and resentment, the puppet wants to know, "Where's the dreams that I've been after?" The puppet never imagined that the drug would take him down. Quite the contrary, he expected it to take him higher. The master had seduced him with the lines "Taste me you will see / More is all you need." The malevolence calls to mind the Satanic seduction in Black Sabbath's classic "N.I.B.," in which the devil instructs his prey to "Look into my eyes, you'll see who I am / My name is Lucifer, please take my hand." For the puppet, grand dreams have not only been left unfulfilled, they have been abandoned. By the time the puppet has reached the stage of ritual misery, all that he wants is more of the drug to satisfy his craving. Gone are the dreams of fame and fortune, lost is the hope for love and happiness. In "N.I.B." Lucifer promises, "I will give you those things you thought unreal / The sun, the moon, the stars all bear my seal." Similarly, cocaine promises euphoria and worldly success. The first high was so spectacular that the puppet chases it to no avail. Cocaine might as well have promised the sun, moon, and stars. In the euphoric state that the drug first delivered, the puppet feels supremely in control and masterful. He finds himself funny, charming, smart, and energetic. He is well set to pursue his dreams. However, subsequent use produces pale shadows of the original high, and eventually crosses the line into suffering, and ends in misery.

The verse continues with the angry indictment that "you promised only lies." In this moment of clarity, the puppet sees his strings, realizing that he was promised freedom but has gotten servitude. He was promised an escape from the pain of life. He was promised confidence, charisma, and insight. He was promised that the drug would serve his needs and make his dreams come true. These were lies, false promises. The truth is that he has become (as another song says) a "servant 'til I fall." It is not a military commander, as in "Disposable Heroes," who sends him to his death. Rather, the commander, the master, is inside his own head. The puppet has become a servant to his own overwhelming desire for the drug. In this way, the drug addiction is akin to possession. It inhabits him. In "N.I.B.," Lucifer boasts, "Now I have you with me, under my power / Our love grows stronger now with every hour." The Sabbath song does not depict possession, but it might as well, since it deals with a false love that is really an insidious dependence. In the Metallica song, the puppet's anger momentarily awakens our hope for change.

The puppet's realization and indictment come too late for action, though. The master has become the servant, and there will not be another reversal. The desire for the drug, the internal master, cackles with glee, and the puppet cries out, "Laughter, laughter / All I hear or see is laughter / Laughter, laughter / Laughing at my cries." The situation is far worse than praying to the deaf ears of a dead God. Stony silence would be welcome by contrast. The laughter in response to the puppet's anger signals that the master finds no threat in the indictment. To the contrary he finds it funny, comical that this impotent individual would dare to assert himself. The puppet could respond by getting angrier and taking action to regain control, but, as we know, that will not happen in this case. The master's laughter foretells the puppet's fate, calling to mind Sabbath's "War Pigs," which concludes with a chilling image: "Satan laughing spreads his wings."

As the verse gives way to guitar, Hetfield screams something unclear. The words were not listed in the lyrics that accompanied the record in 1986, and so they were the subject of debate between my friend Joe and me for years. I heard "freeze frame" and Joe heard "ace of spades." We were both wrong. The actual words make much more sense. Hetfield cries out, "Fix me." In the language of drug culture, the puppet desires a "fix" in the form of the drug. Once the addict has become dependent on the drug, he goes into withdrawal when the drug isn't in the body for a period of time. The drug is required not to get high, but to get fixed—just to feel normal and stop the pain of withdrawal. It works, at least for a short time. Anyone who has ever found relief from a hangover with a Bloody Mary or some other hair of the dog knows it works.

Hetfield's words also connect "Master of Puppets" to "Leper Messiah," in which you "need your Sunday fix," comparing drug dependency to religion, the opiate of the masses. The Sunday service no longer gets you high the way it once did, but it does at least ease your suffering.

There is, though, another way to hear the puppet's cry to "fix me." The words come from the moment of clarity in which he realizes that the master's promises were only lies, that the drug will not deliver success and charisma, that instead it deals in pain and dependence. So, rather than wanting more of the drug for a fix, the puppet may be crying out for help. He has been broken by the drug and wants someone to fix him, to get him off the drug. The request does not seem to be aimed at God or some friend or authority. No one is there to hear it or understand it, after all. Instead, the puppet's request is aimed at himself. The master, the desire for the drug, is internal, issuing from his own body and mind. He has seen the strings, and he would like to cut them. For a moment at least, he has taken the first step, admitting he has a problem. Other people can help him to address the problem, but he will need to follow through on his first step. Sadly, many addicts toggle back and forth between acceptance and denial of the problem. For some, the problem seems too overwhelming, too much to truly fix. This appears to be the puppet's fate.

Kicking the drug and getting sober would require feeling worse before feeling better, and it would take a lot of work. So, retreating behind a wall of denial, the puppet marches to the master's tune. The next verse begins, "Hell is worth all that, natural habitat." Previously the puppet's existence was described as a "life *of* death." Now it is described as "hell," calling to mind the angry indictment from "Dyers Eve" in which the narrator asks his parents, "What is this *hell* you have put me through" and goes on to label them "Believer / Deceiver." For the puppet life may be hell, but the blame cannot find an external target. The puppet himself was the believer in the drug's promises and he, himself, has been the deceiver. Self-deception has trapped him in hell. As in "One," the narrator finds that the torture of his own mind has "left me with life in hell." It is not a matter of devils and pitchforks or even other people. Hell is the mundane existence of feeding a habit that shuts out everything else and that no longer brings real pleasure. The vicious cycle of scoring the drug, using the drug, and needing more of the drug has become the puppet's "natural habitat." It has become pointless, yet self-sustaining, at least for as long as the body can survive the abuse.

Gone are the dreams of happiness and success. There is no higher purpose. Life is "just a rhyme without a reason." The puppet continues to need a fix in the form of the drug, but he has given up on getting fixed. He cannot see a way to exit this "never-ending maze" to walk among the living as he did before he succumbed to the master's invitation to "taste me you will see." It is as if he is sentenced to roam, to "drift on numbered days." His life is coming to an end—his days are numbered, but he does not know the number. An overdose could take him any day, as could violent death in some seedy circumstance.

The master declares, "Now your life is out of season." We understand immediately that this remark is not a promise of safety; the puppet is not like a buck who has survived deer season. Rather, it is a promise of peril. Whether intentionally or not, the line calls to mind The Byrds' famous lyrics "There is a season (turn, turn, turn) . . . / A time to be born, a time to die." For the puppet, the season to be born and to live has come to an end. It is now time to die. The Byrds paraphrased their lines from the Old Testament book of Ecclesiastes (3:1–8), a book which also claims that all human strivings are mere vanity and chasing after wind (1:14). This pessimistic note, absent from The Byrds' "Turn! Turn! Turn!," fits well with the Metallica song.

"Master of Puppets" concludes with the master speaking in the first person, promising, "I will occupy." The imagery calls to mind demonic possession. Not only will the desire for the drug obsessively occupy the puppet's mind, but it will essentially take over. Think here of "N.I.B." and Lucifer's malevolent promise to his beloved that she'll be "forever with me 'til the end of time." The Sabbath song speaks more of damnation than possession, but the point is clear: you've lost control to something that you now wish did not control you. For good reason, hard liquors are called spirits, and some people speak of "demon rum." The person in the grips of an alcohol addiction can seem possessed, even if not literally. He does terrible and tragic things while drunk that he would never do while sober, and often he doesn't even remember doing them. A similar sort of "possession" is at play in drug addiction.

The verse continues, "I will help you die." It's chilling to think that death may be what the puppet actually wants, even if he has not admitted or recognized that desire. Drug use can be a form of subtle suicide. The addict wants to die; he just doesn't want to kill himself directly. The master seems to be reading the puppet's mind when he offers to "help" him die, as if it were a mercy killing, compassionate euthanasia. We need to recall, though, that the master's voice comes from inside the puppet's head. There is no one outside pulling his strings. It is the puppet's own desire for the drug that is dancing him towards death.

Whereas Lucifer promises love and togetherness in "N.I.B.," the master does not tell pretty lies at the end. Instead, he says, "I will run through you." There will be nothing gentle or peaceful about death. The imagery calls to mind the line from "Disposable Heroes" in which the soldier boy is described as "running blind through killing fields." The soldier's death will be violent. Likewise, the puppet's death will be tumultuous. His desire for the drug will not relent; it will only speed up. It will tear through him and rip out all that remains of decency and humanity.

The master's narration concludes with the triumphant statement "Now I rule you too." Any trace of self-control is gone, and all hope is lost. If it were just this one poor puppet who was affected, the story would be sad but not scary. The master's statement makes clear, however, that this puppet is just one victim among many in the past, present, and future.

The topic of self-destructive addiction clearly fascinated Hetfield in 1986, though he does not seem to have identified with it consciously at that time. "Master of Puppets" comes across as a warning about drug addiction, from which Hetfield counted himself safe. There might even be something smug in the songwriter's depiction of the drug addict as a puppet, pulled around by his own foolish desires. By this time, though, Hetfield's alcohol consumption was already legendary and troublesome. Riding a wave of success, he could tell himself that alcohol fueled his creativity and was a necessary part of his lifestyle. Much later in "Frantic," he would recognize that "my lifestyle determines my deathstyle." We need to wonder, though, if Hetfield might have had a nagging suspicion that his drinking was controlling him even at this early date. Writing about drug addiction, a problem he did not have (at least at the time), may have been a safe way to explore a problem he sensed he might have—alcohol addiction. Of course, Hetfield probably would not have consciously recognized this strategy, but it seems plausible in retrospect.

By the mid-1990s, Hetfield's drinking was taking its toll on his relationships with family and friends, and on *Load* we get the first lyrics of self-reflection about alcohol abuse. One song stands out for its engagement with the issue: "The House Jack Built." (The title alludes to Jack Daniel's whiskey on this interpretation. A drug-based interpretation could take the title to allude to "jacking up" or injecting heroin.) In "The House Jack Built" addiction is not presented as a relentless master. Rather, a sense of passivity, inevitability, and hopelessness pervades the lyrics. This is not a song in celebration of someone who enjoyed the booze-soaked good times, like Johnny in "Shooting Star" by

Bad Company, and who "died one night, died in his bed / Bottle of whiskey, sleeping tablets by his head." It's not that kind of cliché. Rather, "The House Jack Built" presents the fatalistic sense of a recurring pattern from which the narrator cannot escape and does not really want to escape.

The song starts with house imagery: "Open door, so I walk inside." The key word is "so." An open door can be a sign of welcome, and it certainly can create curiosity. However, we don't enter every open door we see in life. There is a big difference between a door that has been left open on purpose to welcome us into friendly or familiar circumstances, and a door that is left open to tempt or trick us. We need to exercise caution. Thus one reading of the first line is that it stands for taking the first drink of one's life with no real reflection on what might happen. The drink was there, so I drank it.

As the verse continues, though, a different interpretation of the line becomes clear. This is not the very first time the narrator has taken a drink. Quite the contrary. A pattern has been established, and the narrator can't imagine doing anything different. The force of the word "so" suggests there is no other genuine possibility. The consequences are both desired and dreaded. Having taken the bottle in hand, the narrator says, "Close my eyes, find my place to hide." Will he close his own eyes? Or will his eyes be closed by the drink? The line is richly ambiguous, and both possibilities might be right. He is closing his own eyes to the world outside, and he is willingly taking the drink that will close his eyes further to the world outside. He does not wish to see the world the way it is. Intoxication will provide a "place to hide" both from the world outside and from himself. Though the place may have felt safe once upon a time, it no longer does. With the open door, the open bottle, "I shake as I take it in." The narrator may be shaking from alcohol withdrawal. Once a person has become physically dependent on alcohol, they may get "the shakes" when it is not in their system. The physical trembling impels the alcoholic to drink the morning after a night of debauchery.

In addition to the physical shaking, though, the narrator seems to metaphorically shake with fear at the thought of what may follow once he takes the drink. He will not be content to simply calm his nerves and still his shaky hands. Once he puts alcohol in his system he will wake the sleeping tiger, the relentless and irresistible craving for more and more. He is choosing to lose control in a shameful way. Recognizing the inevitable, the narrator says, "Let the show begin." The out-of-control behavior that will follow may be comic or it may be tragic, but either way it will be pathetic. He will put on a show for others and for himself, creating a spectacle. He knows that he will soon be acting irresponsibly and foolishly. He may enjoy it in the moment, but he will have to wake the next day to the consequences and face himself at least for a moment before beginning the cycle anew. Fear of his uncontrollable actions and the inescapable cycle causes him to metaphorically shake as he pours the booze down his gullet.

As the alcohol fuels his system, the narrator describes himself as "well on my way, but on my way to where I've been." He is drinking to achieve an effect, to get somewhere, to lose his ordinary sense of self, and to stop feeling the pain of the world. When he was new to drinking, the effect was magical, the answer to all his problems. It provided an escape, but now it is a trap—it is the same thing over and over again with only minor variations. Alcohol only takes him to where he has been, to the same old feelings and scenarios. Yet this is what he wants—it is his place to hide. The narrator begins by taking action, walking in the open door, but now action is taken on him: "It swallows me as it takes me in its fog." He began by swallowing the drink, but now the drunken state swallows him. The man takes a drink, and then the drink takes the man. This is no surprise. It is what he wanted, and it is where he has been before. Later in the song the narrator makes his wish clear: "Swallow me so the pain subsides." He wants to ease his pain by being swallowed up by the fog of intoxication.

The image of the fog perfectly depicts the dulled consciousness that is desired. The world's problems and demands are blocked out, unseen through the fog. The relief comes at a cost, though, as self-control is diminished and navigation is compromised. Like a pair of pants on a clothesline in a storm, "I twist away as I give this world the nod." The bit of self-control and self-respect that was hanging on will soon be blown away. The narrator nods, giving his approval to what he has done and what will follow, but he also nods out, losing awareness and ceasing responsibility. Most likely, the actions that follow will be blacked out and irretrievable to memory the next day. The verse begins with the line "Open my eyes just to have them close again." We can read that lyric as a reference to taking an eye-opener, a morning drink that is needed to crawl out of the clutches of a vicious hangover. The drink allows the narrator to function, but it will close his eyes to reality as one drink leads to another and another.

A subsequent verse begins with the same line, slightly altered: "Open my eyes just to have them *closed* once again." This version of the line makes it clear that the narrator is not closing his own eyes but having them closed. The drink does the work, and the narrator becomes explicit about his wish: "Don't want control /

As it takes me down and down and down again." Along with easing pain, the point of drinking excessively is to lose control. The world demands that we play our roles and rein in our impulses. Conforming in this way is exhausting, especially for someone who is not happy with his role. Anger, frustration, resentment, sadness, and shame all build up, and they need release. The narrator needs a way to lose control and act out. The more he drinks, the deeper down he goes, as with loss of inhibition comes loss of clarity.

The imagery of walking in a door sets the stage for the song, and it provides a lens for reading. The poet William Blake famously said that if the doors of perception were cleansed, we would see the world as it is, infinite. The point is that human perception is quite limited. Inspired by Blake and Aldous Huxley, Jim Morrison and company named their band The Doors. True to the experimental spirit of the 1960s, they thought that taking drugs like LSD would eliminate filters on perception and allow them to see the world more truly as it is. In "The House Jack Built" the narrator recognizes that alcohol (and probably other drugs too) actually takes us further away from perceiving reality as it truly is. In fact, distance from reality is one of the costs to be paid for easing pain through the escape of intoxication. Comically but pathetically, the narrator asks, "Is that the moon or just a light that lights this dead-end street?" He is so unable to accurately perceive reality through the foggy lens of drunkenness that he has to wonder whether he is looking at the moon. Though the singing doesn't slur, we can easily imagine the slurred speech of a Falstaffian drunk asking this question. The drunken clown turns poetic philosopher as he wonders if the object of his vision might instead be "just a light that lights this dead-end street." He realizes that he is on a dead-end street, that he is going nowhere literally and metaphorically. The moon is not lighting his way on some noble quest. Rather, he is stumbling along on the brink of losing consciousness, perhaps destined to pass out in an alleyway. This is the course that his life is running.

The verse concludes with another question: "Is that you there or just another demon that I meet?" The narrator is haunted by past misdeeds and people he has wronged. We can imagine him separated from his drinking companions, lost in the back alleys of his own mind, unable to see straight. The effect of chewing on a regret becomes borderline hallucinatory, as he muses on whether it is some phantom of his mind or a real person who emerges from the streetlight.

In contrast to the foggy ruminations of the previous verse, the chorus kicks in with clarity as it reckons with the costs of going through the door of intoxication. As practical experience confirms, "The higher you are / The farther you fall." There is a price to pay for your escape, not just in money frittered away, but in the pain of the hangover. The more you drink tonight, the worse you will feel when you wake tomorrow. This is one reason why a seasoned veteran of the drinking game will not allow himself to come all the way down. Upon waking he will take the morning drink that fends off the hangover. It is not just a matter of dealing with the physical pain of the comedown, though. In the high of the drunken state, the narrator has likely become grandiose, imagining himself to be bigger, stronger, smarter, and more attractive than he really is. Worse, he probably has not contained his grandiosity to his own thoughts, but rather has acted on it, boasting and playing the big shot. Pride goes before the fall, as the proverb says. Waking in pain, puke, and piss the next morning he has fallen from the heights.

The verse continues, "The longer the walk / The farther you crawl." For every action, there is an equal and opposite reaction. You can take the night's escapades as far as the booze will go, but you will have to crawl back to where you started. We can imagine the narrator passing out beneath the light on the dead-end street and needing to crawl back to his home the next morning. More literally, we can imagine him crawling on hands and knees to pray to the porcelain god, to vomit up what poisons his system and soul.

Switching to self-address, the narrator notes, with a sense of irony, "My body, my temple." From a Christian perspective, St. Paul says that your body is the temple of the Holy Spirit (1 Corinthians 6:19). God dwells within you, and so you must not pollute your body. From a broader, more ecumenical perspective, the body may be seen as the temple of the soul. In this sense, what is highest and best, your soul, deserves your body to be not just a home but a temple. The fear is that the soul could be tainted by the body if the body is not kept pure. With reference to his body, the narrator admits, "This temple, it tilts." The drunk tilts, because he literally can't stand up straight, but the effects of alcohol can be chronic. A barroom sense of humor and matter-of-fact acceptance characterize the comment. Drinking takes its toll on the body, and there is no use in denying it—there are plenty of other problems to deny. This body is no temple. Rather, the narrator invites us to "step into the house that Jack built." The phrase transforms the title of the traditional child's story "The House That Jack Built." In the Metallica song, the phrase becomes an easy play on the kind of T-shirt slogan that reads, say, "Body by Budweiser" as it stretches over a beer belly. In this case, the body is the house that Jack Daniel's built. The famous Tennessee whiskey was not Hetfield's preferred liquor (vodka was), but it stands in well for alcohol in general. This body is home not to the Holy Spirit, but to spirits of the alcoholic variety. It is not with pride that the narrator calls his body the house that Jack built. Instead, he recognizes that he has become a physical wreck befitting the damage he has done to himself, to his mind, through drinking.

In a variation on earlier lines, the narrator explains, "Open door, yes, I walk inside / Swallow me so the pain subsides / And I shake as I take the sin." The open door, the bottle, the choice to drink confronts him. We would hope that he would walk away. After all, he seems to realize the damage he has done to himself and the consequences that will follow if he persists. As if in answer to our question—"Will you?"—he replies, "Yes, I walk inside." Why? Because he does not have any other effective way to deal with life. He wants intoxication to "swallow" him "so the pain subsides." The pain will not disappear, but it will diminish, though only temporarily and only at a price. A subtle shading changes the original line from "I take it in" to "I take the sin." Dishonoring your body is a sin in the Christian sense because your body is not ultimately yours, but God's. The narrator may not see the sin quite so literally, but he does recognize that taking alcohol into his body is not a good long-term strategy for dealing with the pain of life. He is sinning in the sense of wasting his life. He would rather live differently, but he experiences himself as a sinner who does not have the strength to choose what is better for him. Really, he can't see his way to a better life.

The closing verse recaps his cyclical misery. In clipped form, we get "Open my eyes / It swallows me / Is that you there." This is the pattern he is doomed to repeat. His eyes will literally and metaphorically open and close with the intake of alcohol. For a time, it will have the desired effect of swallowing him, taking away the pain and the tortured sense of self. Lost in the landscape of his mind, he will mull over the past. The question "Is that you there?" strikes a faint note of hope when it is decoupled from the question that follows in the lyrics: "Or just another demon that I meet?" Maybe the narrator imagines there is someone from the past who could rescue him and show him the way out of his misery. If there is hope, it does not last long. The lyrics conclude, "I twist away / Away / Away / Away." The imagery stays with us as the music fades out. The body that Jack has built is twisted and gnarled, battle-scarred from alcohol abuse. Even worse, the narrator's train of thought has become so twisted that he cannot see a way of straightening out. He is twisted in his own thoughts of "poor mistreated me" ("Poor Twisted Me"). *Poor me, poor me*, has become *pour me another drink so that I can forget about my thoughts and lose control of my actions.*

But why? The perplexing thing for anyone who has ever lived through addiction or watched as a loved one suffered through it, is why self-knowledge does not suffice. Clearly, it does not. The narrator, like many other alcoholics and addicts, realizes that he has a problem, but he is not going to take steps to solve it. Instead, he is going to "twist away." If human beings were purely logical and rational, addiction (and many other problems) would be easily solved. Because we are not purely rational or logical, we need to walk a mile in the shoes of the addict to get a sense of what the struggle is like.

"Low Man's Lyric" from *Reload* can give us a sense of that struggle. The song begins with the contrasting lines "My eyes seek reality / My fingers seek my veins." The narrator is torn. One part of him wants to understand and admit his obvious problem; his eyes seek reality. Another part of him wants to deny and hide from the problem; his fingers seek veins for injection. Just understanding and admitting the problem will not solve it. Taking the drug will make the worry and pain disappear for the moment. It's clear that the drug is the easier and quicker solution. Maybe his eyes are winning against his fingers for the moment, because the first verse concludes, "There's a dog at your back step / He must come in from the rain." The narrator has hurt and disappointed people who love him, but there is someone who still cares. Eliciting sympathy, the narrator depicts himself as a dog who has been caught in the rain. Not quite a stray, but not really a house pet either, the dog has come seeking shelter. It's hard to imagine joy at his return, though. This dog may have its tail between its legs, but it's been back before. This is not the prodigal son, whose return might be celebrated for the change of heart it signals. Instead, this is the dog who returns periodically when the weather gets too rough.

Flashing back to the circumstances that catalyze the return, the narrator says, "The trash fire is warm / But nowhere safe from the storm." We get a scene of urban decay where homeless people camp and keep warm by fires burning in trash barrels. If they huddle really close, it's warm enough by the fire, but that heat will not suffice when the wind and the rain start blowing. Of course, the physical setting is meant to mirror the emotional setting. The drug provides warmth and comfort but only to a limited extent. Once the storms of life set in, the drug isn't nearly enough. When the eyes seek reality, they find an unwelcome sight in self-reflection: "And I can't bear to see / What I've let me be / So wicked and worn." The fingers feel for the veins because the drug obscures the hard truth of personal decline. In self-reflection, for the moment, there is personal responsibility, as the narrator tacitly admits that he has let himself become this way, wicked and worn. His integrity has been compromised. In need of the drug and under the influence of the drug, he has done things he never thought he would. He has not just done wicked things, but through repeated actions has become wicked. Yes, he could become good again, but it would not be easy. Undoing bad habits would take time and take work. In the past, perhaps years ago, he could hide his wickedness behind a respectable appearance. Now, though, there is no mask that could cover how worn he has become. So the thought of returning to someone who cares about him is too painful. He can kid himself, but the truth will be written on his weathered face. The other person will see it and reflect it back to him in her eyes.

It seems there is nowhere to go. The need for a moment of truth bursts forth as "I cry to the alleyway / Confess all to the rain." Rather than keep it all bottled up, the narrator admits his pain and troubles publicly, yet in a way that no one will notice. In a sense it seems that is what Hetfield himself is doing through this song. He is confessing his own pain and his struggle with drinking, not by admitting it forthrightly to someone who cares but by cloaking it in the obscurity of a song about a homeless drug addict. That way Hetfield feels some of the cleansing effect of a confession, but without any of the serious consequences and without doing something to repair the problem. He may not have been aware this was what he was doing at the time of writing the lyrics, but it probably seems that way considered in retrospect. And likely much more than just this one Hetfield song would fit in the category of confessing to the rain.

There is something nearly universal about this mode of operation, confessing indirectly. We're not talking about Freudian slips, where the unconscious comes bubbling forth. Instead "confessing all to the rain" is a way of telling people who wouldn't understand. It can also be a way of telling people who would understand, but telling them in terms they don't understand. Confession is good for the soul, as wise people have always known. Some religions make it a regular part of their practice. Catholicism, for example, makes a sacrament of it. Traditionally, Catholics have confessed their sins to a priest who is behind a screen so that he cannot see the face of the sinner. The practice does not guarantee anonymity, but in a way that is better. There is something close to complete secrecy and anonymity without an absolute guarantee. In the song, the narrator admits his wrongs and regrets in an alleyway, a place even the homeless denizens have abandoned in search of better shelter. So who will hear him? Most likely no one, and yet anyone could. Sometimes people are more daring when confessing in plain sight, though you need to read between the lines to learn what they really mean. It's not that they want to get caught or found out, but they want the thrill of possibly being exposed together with the dual relief of confession and escape.

A confession that does not demand accountability has little lasting effect, however. If, instead of crying to the alleyway, the narrator had admitted his wrongs and regrets to a person who cared, the person would have asked what he planned to do to set things right. With no one to hold him accountable in this way, the narrator retreats. As usual, he finds refuge in self-deception. The lines that follow the confession show how quick and powerful the self-deception is: "But I lie, lie straight to the mirror / The one I've broken to match my face." The confession is cathartic, but then fear sets in with the realization of the hard road forward. So the narrator does the seemingly impossible, he immediately lies to himself. How can that possibly work? Hetfield's poetic explanation is perfect: the narrator has broken the mirror to match his face. On the literal level, the image suggests a mirror that has been warped to favor his face. We all have mirrors we like because the lighting and the angles flatter us—and there are certainly mirrors we avoid for their unflattering tendencies. Of course, what is meant in the song is that the narrator has broken and warped the tools of introspection such that they justify his actions. Perhaps he blames someone else for his circumstances, denies that things are as bad as they seem, or promises to take action if some future threshold is crossed. As with the inclination to "confess all to the rain," the inclination to break the mirror of self-reflection is nearly universal. We skew our self-assessments to avoid the kind of honest self-appraisal that might demand action.

Despite his situation, the narrator is remarkably free of self-pity. Or, at least, he doesn't want pity from anyone else because he does not see himself as a victim. Nonetheless, the narrator's thoughts turn to a person who may still care about him. Actually, though, they are more than just thoughts. Hetfield sings, "So as I write to you / Of what is done and to do." The narrator is not writing a letter, and so the only one writing anything is Hetfield writing lyrics. All the more then, the song seems to be Hetfield's confession. The next line pushes this interpretation further: "Maybe you'll understand / And won't cry for this man." He's not writing something that is clear and transparent. Still, someone may get it. If you do get it, though, he doesn't want sympathy. Who is "you"? Maybe Hetfield's wife. But if the "you" turns out to be the song's listener, don't feel badly for him. Why? "'Cause low man is due." The narrator is the "low man" of the title. There is no victim mentality here.

The low man is not someone wronged by society, not someone who is simply down on his luck. Such people exist, but the narrator does not see himself as one of them. In the song's second verse he explains, "I fall 'cause I've let go / The net below has rot away." According to the imagery of his descent, he was not pushed. Rather, he let go. Ultimately, it was his choice and responsibility that led him to fall into his sordid life. Indeed, he sees his life and his person as foul, indicated in the lines "Touch clean with a dirty hand / I touch the clean to the waste." He has polluted himself, and he pollutes what he touches. There may have once been a safety net to break his falls, but that is gone, rotted away through time. He really doesn't want to be the rain dog seeking shelter from the storm. He doesn't want to pollute the life and dwelling of the person who may still care. Instead, he adds, as a coda to the verse, "Please forgive me." He's not asking directly; he's not begging forgiveness face to face from the person he has wronged. Rather, he's wishing for forgiveness by writing for it in this song. He wants forgiveness in order to gain a sense of peace, rather than for a grand reunion and reconciliation. As he pleads, it seems that he is addressing not just the other person but also himself. Though the narrator does not suffer from self-pity, he does feel great guilt. He blames himself for what he has become, "so wicked and worn," and he would like to be forgiven. If he could forgive himself, then his eyes might be able to seek reality without his fingers seeking veins.

The fingers win the fight for now, and the narrator winds up in a precarious position: "So low, the sky is all I see." The image is a riddle. If you're so low, why can you only see what is high, the sky? The answer: you're on your back. If you've been brought low to your knees, you see what is even lower, the ground beneath you. If, though, you've been knocked flat on your back, when you look up, the sky is all you see. Because you are unsheltered, you don't see a ceiling, you see the sky. The sight is not a delight; you are not cloud-gazing on a summer afternoon. Instead, you are coming to, outdoors on a winter morning. You don't belong there, no one does. You'll freeze to death. The narrator exclaims, "All I want from you is forgive me." Desperation moves him forward with hope and silent promises of reform.

As the song ends, we return to the image of the dog waiting at the back step. Whether the person who lives there forgives the narrator or not, she at least takes pity on him: "So you bring this poor dog in from the rain." The sight of the wretched creature, the low man, moves her heart no matter how many times he has broken it before. Does she dare to hope? Does she forgive him? Whether she does or not, it makes no difference, because "he just wants right back out again." The cycle will not end until he breaks free of the chains of addiction or dies. The song echoes with the somber sound of a funeral dirge, and the final lines are "My eyes seek reality / My fingers seek my veins." So we do not leave the low man with a hope for longevity. He seems "hardwired to self-destruct."

The song "Hardwired" focuses on the chaotic state of the world, but we can get a sense of what it means for an addict to be hardwired to self-destruct by considering a song from *St. Anger* called "Sweet Amber." Composed in collaboration with Kirk Hammett, the song offers reflections on alcohol addiction from a newly sober James Hetfield. Coincidentally, "Sweet Amber" continues the dog imagery of "Low Man's Lyric." In this case, though, the dog is not the bedraggled creature who shows up at the back step. Rather, the dog is the befuddled pet who does whatever he is told: "Chase the rabbit, fetch the stick / She rolls me over 'til I'm sick." A good dog does what he is told, even when the games aren't fun anymore, even when they make him vomit. Why? Because the dog wants to please the master (master of puppies, I'm pulling your strings!).

The song's title makes the master a woman, creating the image of a henpecked man who cannot extricate himself from a toxic relationship. The master's name is Amber, and actually she's not a woman at all. She is the amber beverage of beer or whiskey. And the man is not really henpecked and codependent; he's beer-soaked and alcohol-dependent. His brain chemistry has been so warped through the pleasure he associates with drinking that he cannot seem to resist Sweet Amber even though she no longer delivers pleasure reliably. Instead, "she deals in habits, deals in pain." The ordinary and expected response would be to avoid the source of such misery, but that's not what the dog does, at least not permanently. Instead, the narrator says, "I run away but I'm back again."

Running away from an abuser makes sense, but why does the dog return? That's the mystery. Is he biologically hardwired to self-destruct? In that sense, is he genetically predisposed to addiction? Or has his brain chemistry just been warped by excessive drinking and its initial association with pleasure? Maybe it's ultimately a matter not of biology, but of psychology. Maybe a whole constellation of circumstances conspired to push him back repeatedly to the source that promises pleasure yet delivers pain. Most likely, it is a combination of biology and psychology that explains the sad predicament.

Whatever the ultimate explanation, the narrator senses that he is caught. He can run away, but he always comes back again. And it is not the master's goal to keep him alive. Her dogs are disposable, and she'll move on to the next one when he's dead. The dog is smart enough to realize that he does not have nine lives and that he's lost control of his own story. Sweet Amber is in charge of telling the tale. "She holds the pen that spells the end / She traces me and draws me in." Sweet Amber is sketching the dog and dictating the story with its grim ending. The pen is not just a writing tool; it's also the cage in which the dog is trapped. Worse, the pen is suggestive of a needle, as the addict may have escalated from imbibing alcohol to injecting narcotics. Either way, the deadly consequence awaits, as the dog will soon be put to sleep, be put out of his misery. The dog may not yet see the end, but he does see the faulty logic of his fatal attraction. He sings of Sweet Amber in the usual way, asking, "How sweet are you? / How sweet does it get?" But the song concludes with the insight that "it's never as sweet as it seems."

Despite this insight, there isn't much hope for the dog. He knows that it will never be as sweet as the first time and that it will not be as sweet as he imagines it to be or even as sweet as it feels in the moment. He'll be back again. He'll focus on the sweetness and relief that the drink or drug brought in the past. And selective memory will block out the negative consequences. Maybe he'll even form a plan for how it will be different next time. He won't overdo it; he'll walk away before he has to run away. Plans like that aren't likely to work, however. The problem isn't really the amber beverage. It's his craving and insatiable desire for the relief that the bottled solution once delivered.

Unlike Amber's dog, the narrator of "Fixxxer" may have a chance to escape. He realizes that the drug has anesthetized him from the pain of his upbringing and glued together the fractured pieces of his mind. It may not be working very well anymore, but how is he supposed to stop if there is nothing to fix him? The narrator asks, "So tell me, can you heal what father's done? / Or fix this hole in a mother's son? / Can you heal the broken worlds within? / Can you strip away so we may start again?" The addict doesn't really want to carry on the way he is, but he can see no alternative. He would love to start life over with a clean slate, but that seems impossible. The damage has been done. Out of desperation, he may be willing to get off the drug and try treatment. With a note of hope, he asks, "Tell me, can you heal what father's done? / Or cut this rope and let us run?" The image of the rope calls to mind a dog tied up, dejected yet yearning to roam. Or we may think of the impotent puppet who is helplessly aware of his strings. As the verse continues, the addict experiences relief without the drug, but then does something incomprehensible. "Just when all seems fine and I'm pain free / You jab another pin, jab another pin in me." Who is "you"? It's the addict himself. The fault does not lie with some other person pushing pins into voodoo dolls. It's an inside job. The goal is "to fall in love with life again," but only he himself could stop shooting up, and only he could start again. So why? Why, after experiencing relief from pain without the drug, does he return to it? As the song concludes, the narrator pleads, "No more pins in me / No more, no more pins in me." If he continues to think that the problem is caused by outside forces and can only be healed by outside forces, he's unlikely to succeed in staying sober and falling in love with life again.

With time away from drinking or drugging the addict may be inclined to think that the problem has been solved and that the reset button has been pushed. He can begin anew with a clean slate. Unfortunately, this does not usually work out well once a person has crossed the line into addiction. There is no turning a pickle back into a cucumber. Consider "Cure" from *Load*, a song that tells the tale of a guy who tries drinking again but finds that problems persist. The narrator describes the drinker, saying, "He thinks the answer's cold and in his hand / He takes his medicine / The man takes another bullet / He's been fooled again." In this lyric, we may have another moment of "confessing all to the rain." From the late 1980s into the 1990s, Hetfield drank Coors Light, known as the Silver Bullet because of its packaging in silver cans. Presumably this beverage seemed like a safe and friendly alternative to stronger stuff. The can may have been silver, but the liquid is practically see-through. No lovely amber color or rich flavor. Of course, Hetfield also drank other beers and vodka at this time, but it must have seemed to him like he was on his good behavior when drinking Coors Light. He may have seen himself as doing penance or curing a problem, as "he takes his medicine." No one wants to take medicine, but it's worth it if it cures you. The cold can may have seemed like the silver bullet that would solve his problems. He needed to drink, but he also needed to get his drinking under control. If he could just stick to this light stuff, at least most of the time, he wouldn't get out of control in a way he would later regret. It makes sense from a certain line of reasoning. The problem is, though, for an alcoholic, one drink leads to another, and while he may start out on Silver Bullets, he's likely to switch to something harder as the drinking session stretches on.

When the drinking session inevitably goes wrong, the drinker realizes "he's been fooled again." Who fooled him? Maybe someone suggested that he stick to Silver Bullets. That's the kind of advice that a friend or manager might offer. If, however, that experiment, that cure, failed once or twice before, who is fooling him now? He's not been fooled. Rather, he's fooling himself. In fact, the drinker may realize he's been fooling himself. He may even have tried abstaining from alcohol for weeks or months in order to push the reset button. So what is he supposed to do now that he realizes he can't drink normally? He realizes that Coors

Light is not the silver bullet that will solve his problem. It's not the cure. From past experience he knows that abstaining from alcohol makes him miserable, and he knows that one drink will temporarily wipe away the misery. The advice to stick to Coors Light may have come from a well-meaning friend or manager, but now other people may be offering different advice. Other people may have another cure in mind.

The narration switches to the point of view of the drinker as Hetfield sings, "Betting on the cure / 'Cause it must get better than this / Betting on the cure / Everyone's got to have the sickness / 'Cause everyone seems to need the cure / Precious cure." The new cure is unspecified, but the guy is willing to take a chance on it because he is miserable, white-knuckling his way through not drinking. He doesn't like the cure—he mocks it as the "precious cure." It's definitely not as palatable as Coors Light, and he definitely doesn't like being preached to about it. People are coming out of the woodwork as evangelical advocates for the cure. They've had the "sickness" too, and they know the cure. So what is it? We can only speculate, but one likely answer is 12-step recovery.

For a skeptical person, recovery groups and programs can certainly seem like cults. They ask you to do and accept all kinds of things that may rub you the wrong way, admitting you are powerless over alcohol and having faith that a higher power can restore you to sanity. With a mix of mockery and anger, the narrator portrays the preachers of sobriety as mindless cult members, "Uncross your arms / Take and throw them to the cure, say, / 'I do believe.'" If fervent adherence to a creed is the cure, then it may be worse than the sickness.

As we know, Hetfield achieved sobriety prior to the release of *St. Anger*. There is no complete cure for addiction, though.

Recovery depends upon maintaining a program one day at a time. When Hetfield returned to drinking in 2019, after 15 years of abstinence, he discovered that he was not able to control it. As a result, Metallica's tour of Australia was cancelled. Thankfully, James found his way back to rehab and sobriety. We can now look forward to glimpsing the lessons he learned through lyrics of songs to come.

# CHAPTER 3

# INSANITY AND CONFUSION

## *Home, Where They Whisper Things into My Brain*

Inspired by *One Flew Over the Cuckoo's Nest*, "Welcome Home (Sanitarium)" speaks to all of us who have ever felt imprisoned, whether we've been confined by the walls of an institution or not. The chorus is repeated a couple of times, but otherwise the narrator tells the story straight through, beginning with the lines "Welcome to where time stands still / No one leaves and no one will / Moon is full, never seems to change." The setting is bleak. The inmates are there for life, and nothing in their environment changes, making it seem as if they are caught in a time warp, cut off from the outside world. The moon is always full—things are always crazy. Abnormal behavior is the norm both among the patients and the staff. The patients, though, are "labeled mentally deranged." The labeling is pernicious because it delegitimizes the thoughts and ideas of those who are labeled. With a clear hierarchy and division between those who are supposedly sane and those who are labeled insane, mistreatment becomes justified. The song is specific in its setting, but it is universal in its appeal.

The narrator is stuck, yet, like (nearly) all of us, he yearns to escape. Waking life in the asylum is a nightmare, so he finds refuge where he can "Dream the same thing every night / I see our freedom in my sight / No locked doors, no windows barred." The inmate literally dreams of leaving, just walking out the door or going out the window—in his dream they aren't locked or barred, and he is free to depart. Importantly, his dream goes beyond mere physical freedom. It includes "no things to make my brain seem scarred." The tests, the treatments, the conditions all make it seem like he is insane, make it look like he has a permanent disfigurement, a scar, not on his face but on his brain. Somehow, he has retained enough presence of mind and self-awareness to realize that although he may be temporarily troubled, he is not permanently damaged.

Speaking to a new arrival, the narrator explains his coping strategy: "Sleep my friend and you will see / That dream is my reality." He is not saying that he is delusional and that he can't tell the difference between dreams and reality. Rather, the narrator is saying that his dreams reflect a greater truth, that he is not insane and that he can envision a reality in which he is free again. Yes, he may literally dream these things while asleep in bed at night, but he also dreams of these things in the metaphorical sense—he envisions and plans and hopes for them in his waking moments. Nonetheless, the narrator is not at peace. Understandably, he is frustrated by his captivity. He is angry, and the staff interpret his anger as a sign of his insanity. "They keep me locked up in this cage / Can't they see it's why my brain says 'rage.'" The staff are perpetuating the problem, even making it worse. Why can't they see that and stop? Probably because the staff have not been taught to recognize the way a sane man would react to insane conditions. Instead, the inmate's anger, his rage, is taken as just one more sign of his insanity.

Sometimes institutions cause the very problems they are supposed to cure. An important precursor and likely influence on "Welcome Home (Sanitarium)" is the 1983 song "Institutionalized" by Suicidal Tendencies, in which the narrator protests against his parents' plan to send him away for help. In spoken-word style, the singer, Mike Muir, delivers these memorable lines: "My best interest? How do you know what my best interest is? / How can you say what my best interest is? What are you trying to say, I'm crazy? / When I went to your schools, I went to your churches, / I went to your institutional learning facilities? / So how can you say I'm crazy?" This narrator is troubled, but he feels certain that being sent to an institution is not the proper solution to his troubles. After all, it was his negative reaction to other institutions—school and churches—that landed him in this state. He just wants to be left alone. Famously, the narrator says, "All I wanted was a Pepsi." If his mother would have just given him a Pepsi and left him alone in his room, maybe things would have worked out. We get a similar sentiment in the chorus of the Metallica song, as the narrator pleads, "Sanitarium, leave me be / Sanitarium, just leave me alone." We can imagine the narrator making this plea before being institutionalized, insisting that he does not need to be locked away from society. But within the context of the song, the narrator seems to be asking the staff within the asylum to cease treating him.

In the Hippocratic Oath, doctors pledge first to do no harm. Historically, most medical care has been risky, and so the best treatment has often been no treatment. Let the body heal itself. The same applies to the care of the mind. We need to beware the possibility that treatment for mental or emotional problems could do more harm than good. Clearly, that is what the narrator believes about his own case. If the only tool a person has is a hammer, every problem looks like a nail. Likewise, the staff of the sanitarium have a limited set of tools and see all problems as solved with the tools in hand. Not all patients are well served. So if the narrator cannot get released or cannot escape, then he just wants to be left alone to let his mind heal itself.

Unfortunately, the staff have other plans for him. They interpret his desire to cease treatment as just one more sign of his insanity. And rather than ready him for a future in which he will be released, they undermine his confidence: "Build my fear of what's out there / Cannot breathe the open air / Whisper things into my brain / Assuring me that I'm insane." The inmate is vulnerable, and his confidence is fragile. He wants to believe that he can overcome the troubles that led to his institutionalization, but the staff only discourage him. They may be malicious or they may be well-meaning, but the results are the same. The messages they send suggest that the inmate is now, and always will be, incapable of living successfully in society.

Few of us have had the experience of this kind of mistreatment in a mental institution, but many of us can think of personal examples from other institutions. We can think, for example, of the implicit, and sometimes explicit, messages from teachers that we were unfit. Some teachers are obviously sadistic in their verbal abuse of students, but others are more subtle. Here Hetfield's line "Whisper things into my brain" speaks volumes. We can all relate to the experience of having an authority figure—teacher, parent, priest, rabbi, coach— who signals to us that we are deficient in some significant way. Subtle and insidious in this abuse, they put thoughts in our heads that we are no good—broken, deficient, subpar. This kind of signaling is pervasive, and it isn't always intentional.

Instead, it can be an institution's culture that leads authority figures to see people in their care through lenses that magnify and even distort perceived deficiencies.

Unfortunately, all too often, we internalize the perceptions others have of us. In the context of the song, the result for the narrator is "assuring me that I'm insane." He has resisted his mistreatment by dreaming of escape, but for the moment his resistance is worn down. He is compelled to think that the staff may be right, that he may indeed be insane and that perhaps the asylum is where he belongs. If he comes to believe this fully, then his chances of acclimating to life outside will be poor. If he is ever released, he will doubt his own ability to live in society and will sabotage his own freedom by taking actions that will return him to the asylum. He will have become institutionalized in the sense of preferring to live within the familiar confines of the sanitarium. This phenomenon occurs among prison inmates who become institutionalized and prefer life in prison, which they know how to navigate, to life in society, which becomes too burdensome in its foreign ways.

Institutionalization calls to mind the song's title. Most fans refer to the song as "Sanitarium," but the full title is "Welcome Home (Sanitarium)." For the person who becomes institutionalized, the asylum may be the closest thing they have to a home, a place where they feel safe and secure. For the person who has been an inmate and who is returning once again after a failed attempt to live in society, the greeting "Welcome Home" may be grimly apt. The phrase "welcome home" does not occur in the song's lyrics, though. Instead, the narrator invites us in with the words, "Welcome to where time stands still / No one leaves and no one will." It's less of a greeting and more of a warning, calling to mind the famous instructions from Dante's *Inferno*,

"Abandon all hope, ye who enter." You have a one-way ticket for your tour of hell.

Despite the hopeless words with which Metallica's song begins, the narrator soon summons hope, talking of his dreams of escape. And although the staff label him and discourage him, the narrator is resilient. To every action there is an equal and opposite reaction. Indeed, the narrator is ready to up the ante. Hetfield sings, "They think our heads are in their hands / But violent use brings violent plans." Some of the treatment in the sanitarium may indeed be violent. The staff may be using their "hands" to treat the "heads" of the inmates. Think of straitjacket restraints and forced medications. The narrator momentarily takes the staff's point of view, and in a mocking tone says, "Keep him tied, it makes him well / He's getting better, can't you tell?" Of course, the staff members don't really think that the inmate is getting better. Tying him up does not make him well. It just subdues the inmate for the moment and warns him against future behavior that does not conform to institutional norms. Ideally, the experience of being restrained would make the inmate less likely to misbehave in the future, but in reality, the restraints may simply inspire resentment.

The narrator comes to see himself as the leader of a rebellion, telling his fellow inmates, "No more can they keep us in / Listen, damn it, we will win." Commenting on the staff, the narrator says, "They see it right, they see it well / But they think this saves us from our hell." The implication is that the staff members realize the restraints and other treatments are cruel and ineffective, but the staff still think they are doing the right thing by keeping the inmates locked up. If the inmates were running the asylum, or released back into society, they would make a mess of things. So the staff see themselves as saving the inmates from the living hell they would create if given control. Or at least that's what they tell themselves. The staff must experience some cognitive dissonance as a result of believing contradictory things, and their misguided authoritarian rule cannot bring them peace of mind. Half-blind to the situation they created, the staff fail to appreciate the inmates' level of anger in response to their mistreatment. Earlier in the song, the narrator marvels at the inability of the staff to see his "rage."

By building our sympathy for the narrator, Hetfield has whispered into our brains. At this point we are ready for the narrator to throw off his chains and take vengeance. The song is effective in enlisting our allegiance because we have all had similar, if less severe, experiences. We have put up with repeated mistreatment by an institution or authority figure and have wanted to break free. In real life, we may or may not have rebelled, but the song allows us to rebel vicariously. The narrator returns to the chorus: "Sanitarium, leave me be / Sanitarium, just leave me alone / Sanitarium, just leave me alone." In effect, these words act as a final plea for peace. All the narrator asks is to be set free.

Of course, the staff will not cease treating him as prescribed, and they will not set him free. The result is unsettling and unstable. The status quo is unacceptable, but it is not clear what can be done to change it. No one is going to listen to a person in an insane asylum. His opinion seems by definition insane and thus easily dismissed. Yet, something has to happen, because if there is no chance for rational discourse, then violence becomes a viable option.

The final verse begins with the line "Fear of living on." This is the second time in the song that the narrator references fear. The first time, he spoke of the staff's attempts to "build my fear of what's out there." Those efforts were successful to a certain extent, but he has ultimately resisted. Now the narrator could be speaking of a similar fear, a fear of enduring life in the sanitarium. If we simply pause on this first line of the final verse, it could suggest that the narrator is ready to turn his fear inward and take his own life. We can certainly imagine that as one possible outcome of the scenario. Instead, though, the line is elucidated by what follows. The narrator has not turned inward. Rather he finds camaraderie in the shared anger of his fellow inmates: "Natives getting restless now / Mutiny in the air." The sanitarium is a powder keg ready to blow, though the staff members don't realize it. They have been violent in their mistreatment of the inmates, and their behavior could justify violence in response. The narrator, though, is ready to take things even further.

Poetically, he tells us, "Got some death to do." For the moment, the line is ambiguous—it could still mean that he will take his own life. Contemplating the decision, he says, "Mirror stares back hard." The image in the mirror is not the smiling visage of a deranged madman, but instead the serious face of a man who has been pushed past the breaking point. In his reflection he does not see a man who is incapable of living or who deserves to die. And so, as he prepares to take action, he says, "Kill, it's such a friendly word." Another piece of poetry, this line draws our attention to the sound of the syllable. "Kill" certainly does sound nice compared to "murder." "Kill" starts with a hard "k" sound but ends with a soft "l" sound. The syllable finds its way into the names of places such as Peekskill and Fishkill, in which "kill" comes from the Dutch language, meaning stream. What could be more friendly than a stream? Of course, it's not just the sound of the word "kill" that is friendly at this point. Rather, the idea of killing has become friendly or welcome. Ordinarily, killing is not an idea we like. Even when we kill an animal for food, we do it with some regret for the loss of life. However, under the extreme circumstances described in the song, the idea of killing has become friendly to the narrator. He will direct death at his tormentors, because it "Seems the only way / For reaching out again." We can sympathize. He wants out, and perhaps he deserves to be out—to live free in society. But he feels like a person who has run out of options—feels like he has been painted into a corner.

Anger builds throughout the song, both in the narrator and in the listener, such that by the time he is ready to kill his tormentors we are right there with him—ready to cheer him on and kill vicariously. This is one of the great benefits of fiction: it provides us catharsis. We can identify with a character and experience negative emotions in a cleansing way. After listening to "Welcome Home (Sanitarium)" we are actually less angry. We are exhausted by the identification with the narrator, and we realize that killing was not his best option, was not "the only way / For reaching out again." By killing the staff, he might have experienced a temporary sense of satisfaction, but the predictable result of killing your way out of an institution is that you will wind up back in another, more restrictive institution. On top of that, you are likely to regret the action, not just because you were caught and institutionalized again, but because you realize that it is difficult to live with the deed. Even after the blood on your hands is wiped away with water, the guilt lingers in your mind. At least, if you are sane—and sane is what the narrator claims to be.

Not all institutions are like the one the narrator kills his way out of, but all institutions mark us and require us to play scripted roles. In effect, they label us, telling us what we are and how we are expected to live. Listeners can readily identify with the narrator of "Welcome Home (Sanitarium)" because we all find ourselves imprisoned by institutions even if there are "no locked doors or windows barred" in our case. Society at large and its many agents—homes, schools, churches—are institutions that label us: son, daughter, student, Christian, worker, etc. No doubt, institutions benefit many people, providing a sense of order, purpose, and stability. Too often, though, they demand stultifying conformity that crushes the spirit of the individual. "Welcome Home (Sanitarium)" tells such a story in extreme form.

"Confusion" from *Hardwired . . . to Self-Destruct* tells a similar story, depicting the plight of a soldier returning from war with post-traumatic stress disorder (PTSD). Inspired by the movie *American Sniper*, Hetfield portrays his subject with care, identifying with him in first-person narration: "My life . . . / The war that never ends." The topic is ancient, going back at least as far as Homer's *Odyssey*, with the hero's ten-year journey back home from the Trojan War, during which he is repeatedly blown off course with pit stops that include distractions such as sex and drugs. Maybe the goal is impossible, though. After all, Thomas Wolfe said, "You can't go home again." In other words, home has changed and so have you. In Homer's story, the hero, Odysseus, eventually succeeds, though. He returns to the kingdom of Ithaca in disguise, finds that his wife, Penelope, has been faithful, and slays the suitors who have been courting his wife and drinking his wine. Do Odysseus and Penelope live happily ever after? Homer does not say, but we are led to believe so. Perhaps that is the most unbelievable part of the story.

Even though Odysseus remains physically strong and unscathed, he must be emotionally scarred. Death in battle came from gruesome combat. How many men lost their lifeblood on Odysseus's blade? How many friends did he see reduced to corpses? Yes, death was more abundant in the ancient world: nearly half of all children died before reaching adulthood, and many adults died from infections easily cured today. Meat for the dinner table was slaughtered and butchered by one's own hands. Nonetheless, the gore and horror of the ancient battlefield must have been beyond imagination. By contrast, modern military killing can seem antiseptic. Shooting someone at a distance does not, at first glance, seem as difficult as stabbing someone at close range. In fact, though, the diagnosis of PTSD among returning soldiers is higher now than ever. Admittedly, it may actually have been worse in the past. PTSD was not understood, and soldiers suffering from it were often ridiculed as cowards by commanders and comrades. Even today there is a stigma attached to PTSD, making it difficult for members of the military to seek treatment while in active duty and even afterwards. In ancient times the virtue of courage was so closely associated with battle that physical scars were badges of honor, but emotional scars were sources of shame. Too much of this mentality persists.

We still have a long way to go, but we are making progress towards understanding and accepting the reality of the psychological injuries that soldiers suffer in war. Hetfield honors this progress with his sympathetic depiction of the soldier in "Confusion." Indeed, the soldier suffers confusion upon his return home, and no one really understands.

"Confusion" begins with a martial drumbeat and doom-laden accompaniment. But then, just as we prepare to sink into a dirge, a triumphant riff emerges, promising perseverance and offering hope in the midst of despair. To find the hope, we must face the reality, though: "Coming home from war / Pieces don't fit anymore." The pieces don't fit—the world does not make sense. War makes sense when you're in it, however. There are good guys and bad guys, friends and enemies. The people you are trying to kill are trying to kill you. The intensity and adrenaline rush of war can be addictive, leaving the soldier ill-suited for civilian life. The hypervigilance, the constant state of alert, cannot be easily shut off. As a result, the soldier is "trapped in a memory forever" as "crossfire ricochets inside me." In short, you "Leave the battlefield / Yet its horrors never heal." The body may return home to family with life and breath in it, but the mind may be lost or damaged beyond repair. As the song suggests from the soldier's point of view, "All sanity is now beyond me."

Despite the family's best efforts to love and heal the returning soldier, the results may be discouraging. Imagine the small child who finally gets his daddy back after months or years apart. The stories his mommy tells of his hero don't fit the reality of the man he meets. "Father please come home / Shell shocked all I've known." From the look in his father's eyes, the boy can tell that his father is not really there. The man is stuck somewhere else, even though he slumps in the chair right in front of the boy. A child can't be expected to make sense of the situation or heal his father.

We would hope that other people could comprehend the soldier's situation and render aid, but not so. The situation, as the song depicts it, is bleak: "Label him a deadwood soldier now / Cast away and left to roam / Rapid is the road to sacrifice / Just takes longer to come home." Not even the military itself can find value in him in his current state, or at least that's how it seems to the psychologically scarred soldier. From his perspective, they see him as "deadwood," useless. He is "cast away" like a piece of driftwood to be tossed about on the troubled sea of his own mind. On what shores will he land? Like Odysseus, blown off course from his return after the Trojan War, will our deadwood soldier find solace in sex and drugs? Possibly, but the song doesn't say. Rather, he is "left to roam," like some stray dog. Will he bite? That is the chance society takes.

Long before he became a stray dog, he was a young man ready to serve his country; perhaps he was one of those who eagerly joined the military after the 9/11 attacks. "Rapid is the road to sacrifice," as the song says. What the young man did not realize when he signed up was that "it takes longer to come home." This is an understatement. No doubt, the young man was tough and ready. If he ever envisioned his eventual return, he saw praise and glory with a successful career and a happy life. He did not anticipate the psychological scars, and he did not realize that "war is never done." When he returns, he is not missing a limb and he does not wear a Purple Heart, and so to all appearances he is fine. His erratic behavior seems inexplicable and inexcusable, especially to those who do not know him well.

According to the old saying, you should "be kind, for everyone you meet is fighting a great battle." The power and wisdom of the saying is found in the fact that the battle is not obvious. The battle is not literally a military campaign, of course. In "The Unforgiven" Hetfield employs the life-is-war metaphor: "Throughout his life the same / He's battled constantly / This fight he cannot win." It's almost a cliché, but only because it's true. The language of war is the language of life, with its battles, struggles, triumphs, victories, defeats, surrenders, and so on. We all fight our own private battles, coping with stress and its various causes. We see only the other person's outside and do not know his inside. We would be more sympathetic if we realized the vast, unseen suffering that surrounds us. Even when the war is over, *the war is not over*—we continue to fight to heal and survive. So we might recast the saying as "Be kind, for everyone you meet is returning home from battle." We are all the walking wounded. When we say to a combat veteran, "Thank you for your service," one of the things we must surely be expressing is our recognition that the battle continues because they may never fully heal. Likewise we can recognize that all of us are not only currently fighting unseen battles but still healing from past injuries. We are all trying to make it back home, wherever and whatever home may be.

Certainly, many combat veterans suffer psychological wounds from real battles that make civilian psychological wounds from metaphorical battles seem silly. Indeed, there is an epidemic of suicide among troops returning from Iraq and Afghanistan. Thankfully, though, the soldier in "Confusion" does not give up, as many understandably have.

# CHAPTER 4

# DEATH

*Now that We've Faded to Black under Ice*

"Fade to Black" perfectly captures the loss of self and the loss of hope experienced by a person contemplating suicide. Hetfield is so convincing in his portrayal that fans have easily mistaken him for the narrator of the song. In fact, though, the catalyst for the song was a bit of temporary despair brought on by the theft of some equipment. Hetfield himself was not suicidal.

Rather than encouraging suicide, "Fade to Black" has had the salutary effect of saving fans from suicide. Singing along provides catharsis, a purging of negative emotions. The song offers listeners and fans hope that there is a way out of despair. Indeed, one way out would be the creation of art like "Fade to Black." The song inspires the listener to find some purpose, some reason to carry on.

We can imagine the soldier from "Confusion" taking solace in "Fade to Black." The soldier has realized that "Coming home from war / Pieces don't fit anymore." He may have a house, but he does not have a home; he does not have a coherent sense of self. He looks within and finds only confusion and delusion, concluding, "All sanity is now beyond me." Although suicide is often wrongly seen as a coward's way out, the truth is that the mental pain of depression is worse than any physical pain. Consider that physical pain can be overcome by the mind, whereas the mind itself is no refuge from the pain of depression. We should not be quick to judge the person who has chosen to leave us by his own hand. Certainly, there is hope for recovery from depression, and we should do everything we can to bring that hope and that recovery to the person who is suffering. Part of what is required is removing the stigma from mental suffering and depression. There is nothing shameful in it. Quite the contrary, there is something to be proud of. Those of us who have suffered depression have been wounded on the battlefield of life. Instead of hiding, you should, as Hetfield sings in another song, "show your scars." The emotional vulnerability displayed and encouraged by Hetfield's lyrics is a helpful corrective to the stoic hypermasculinity that can lead a veteran of military combat, or life's war, to feel that suicide is a better option than admitting that one suffers inside.

The lyrics to "Fade to Black" are instructive in their description of the state of confusion and the loss of self. Plaintively, the narrator notes, "Things not what they used to be / Missing one inside of me." It is disorienting to find oneself in unfamiliar circumstances, but it is truly troubling when those circumstances are within one's own mind. At least the narrator can recognize that the situation is not normal, that things used to be different. Despite the imprecise diagnosis of the first line above, the second line is remarkably astute in its observation that the prior sense of self is missing. Presumably, the narrator once had a worldview in which things held together and in which he had a place. He understood how to navigate the terrain of the world because he knew who he was. Now his self-image has been shattered and there seems to be no way to put the pieces together again. This is not a mere curiosity or a bizarre hallucinogenic vision. Rather, the narrator reacts to it, saying, "Deathly loss, this can't be real." He describes the experience of a loss far greater than the loss of a broken heart or the loss of a loved one. And the initial reaction is that it can't be happening. The grieving process for the loss of a loved one or the pain of a broken heart is real and its trigger is clear. What's more, the person grieving in those circumstances will receive pity and compassion. Others will recognize the external cause, and most will identify with the pain and suffering. After all, most people have been through something similar. Not everyone, though, has been through depression, and those who have not suffered from it often have a tough time feeling compassion for the depressed person. They are apt to equate depression with their own experiences of sadness or the blues, and thus they are apt to offer advice to just snap out of it. When the person suffering from depression does not snap out of it, others may become impatient and judgmental, seeing the person as just feeling sorry for himself and willfully wallowing in self-pity.

"Fade to Black" continues, "Cannot stand this hell I feel." The line says more than it may appear to on first glance. The phrase "cannot stand" has been overused to a point where it has lost its power. We may say, for example, that we cannot stand politicians, but what we really mean is that we greatly dislike them. The narrator of the song, though, is talking about a pain so intense that he cannot tolerate it any longer. He is at the point where he will choose to terminate his own existence rather than feel the pain for another moment. He describes the pain as "this hell I feel." In the minds of many, hell is a place of great physical torments, with flames searing flesh. But that hell would be readily endured in exchange for the end of the pain of depression. In fact, people suffering from depression may self-inflict the physical pain of cutting themselves as a way of feeling something different. Of course, some theologians have conceived the suffering of hell as more mental and less physical, a realization of one's separation from God and a sense of regret for the life one has lived that resulted in this damnation. But even that state of mental suffering may sound like a desirable change from the pain of depression.

Depression does have its physical symptoms as well, sometimes manifesting as aches and pains, but more generally as a heaviness and lack of energy. The song continues with the lines "Emptiness is filling me / To the point of agony." The narrator is not brimming over with anger or choked with rage. Rather he is filled with emptiness, a paradoxical description. How can someone be filled with emptiness? Emptiness is the lack of something particular, something we need and take for granted. When you need and expect to find cash, an empty wallet does not just lack cash—it is disorienting in what it denies you. All the more so, when you look within and cannot find the self you once knew and counted on, the result is disorienting and painful—perhaps more like being deprived of oxygen than cash. The narrator describes it as "agony." Imagine the excruciating pain of a kidney stone or childbirth. Part of what allows us to endure such agony is the promise that it will end and that we will be restored to normal. By contrast, depression is characterized by lack of hope in the future. The narrator describes it as "growing darkness taking dawn." The old saying tells us that it is always darkest before the dawn, meaning that we should forebear because things look their worst before they change for the better. This may often be true, but it does not seem true to the person suffering from depression. In this case the darkness is "taking" the dawn, swallowing the hope for a brighter tomorrow. The woman giving birth can at least envision the joy of holding her newborn child at the end of the painful process she is enduring. By contrast, the depressed person sees no positive outcome or future horizon. This is part of what makes depression so difficult to treat. Thankfully, though, depression can be treated, and so it need not be fatal.

In the final line of the verse, the narrator says, "I was me, but now he's gone." Poetically paradoxical, the line leaves us wondering who is speaking. Of course, we know it is still the narrator, but who is he at this point if he is not himself? The answer is that he is a diminished and altered version of his former self. Utter hopelessness is expressed in the belief that "he's gone." This isn't a case of not feeling quite like yourself one day. Rather, this is a matter of having only a memory of what it once felt like to be yourself and reaching the conclusion that the feeling won't return. We can imagine an old man recalling that he once was a great athlete, but those days have gone. The old man is still himself, however. By contrast, the song's narrator has lost something more essential, his sense of himself, his sense of who he is and how he fits into the world.

"Fade to Black" begins with melancholic acoustic guitar leading into the first line, "Life, it seems, will fade away." Upon hearing that line for the first time, one might think the song is simply a reflection on the transitory nature of existence, like "Dust in the Wind," the classic by Kansas. The second line, "Drifting further every day," begins to disrupt that interpretation as the listener is forced to wonder what is drifting. It turns out to be not a *what* but a *who* that is drifting, the narrator himself. It is as if the narrator is a small boat that has been unmoored and is lost in the fog at sea. He describes the experience as "getting lost within myself." This sounds impossible. If there is one place where one should not be able to get lost, it is within oneself, but the experience of depression shows that this condition is quite possible. The constant rumination, questioning, and self-doubt that plague the depressed mind are disorienting. "Know thyself" was written on the wall of the Oracle at Delphi, and Socrates similarly said that the unexamined life is not worth living. What the philosopher forgot to add was that the constantly examined life is unlivable. This is the state of the depressed person; the self-lacerating self-examination becomes unlivable to the point where the healthy sense of self is lost.

Ironically, the depressed person can appear selfish to others. We all have problems and doubts, but we don't let them bog us down. We lean forward into life and make the best of things. For the depressed person, though, "nothing matters, no one else." To say that nothing matters conceals the fact that everything matters. However, when everything matters, nothing really matters. As he drifts and descends, the depressed person is bothered and upset by everything to the point where nothing can make him feel better. Nothing, no piece of good news, can cheer him up, because it seems like a mere drop of water in the empty bucket of despair.

Likewise, no *one* else matters. Contrast this with Hetfield's love song "Nothing Else Matters." When you fall in love, the person you love takes center stage to the extent that all else recedes into the background. Nothing much can bother you. But when you are depressed, that same person, whom you love, ceases to matter. It's not that you can no longer care, but that you can no longer be reached. You're drifting away, and you can hear the voice of love and concern—you just can't feel it. All the more so, other people cease to matter. It's not that you have become suddenly selfish in the sense of being greedy or predatory. It's that you can't get out of your own head, with the result that you lose your sense of self, your pride, your ambition, your purpose. And you begin to believe that other people would be better off without you. Taking stock, the narrator declares, "I have lost the will to live / Simply nothing more to give." The will to live is so basic to human and animal existence that we take it for granted. To lose it is to give up. People suffering from a terminal illness may extend their lives by willing themselves to live, but those who lose the will to live are soon dead. Depression is not necessarily a terminal illness, but it certainly can result in loss of the will to live. However, the depressed person will not simply expire when that will is lost. To bring his life to an end he will need to somehow summon one last act of will.

In describing the situation that has led to losing the will to live, the narrator says, "There is nothing more for me." This kind of magnification and negative forecasting is typical of the depressed mind. It is literally "all or nothing" thinking. The truth is that even for the most depressed person there is something or someone who still matters to some degree and who makes life better to some extent. The depressed mind, though, magnifies the negative and minimizes the positive. It also overgeneralizes and makes only negative predictions for what life will be like in the future. As a result, the mind desires a permanent solution, suicide, to what could be a temporary problem, depression. The narrator declares, "Need the end to set me free." By declaring that he needs the end, the narrator expresses the desire for an end to his pain and suffering. It is not a desire to hurt or punish himself; he would prefer to die passively like a terminally ill patient who has given up the fight to live. There is certainly no desire to do violence to himself. Presumably he would like the simplest and most painless means of bringing the end. If there were a button at the side of his bed that he could push, that would be best. He wants the end "to set me free." Freedom from unendurable pain and suffering is what he seeks. He may be mistaken, however, in thinking that death will set him free.

Death may simply destroy him. If death is the end of all existence, then he will not be set free but erased. Perhaps that is OK, perhaps that is what he chooses. It is virtually impossible to imagine one's own nonexistence, because one always plays spectator to it in one's own mind or imagination. Still, we can suppose that the narrator would rather cease to be than continue in his current existence. If, as Hamlet imagines it might be, death is simply a dreamless sleep, then "'tis a consummation / Devoutly to be wish'd."

"To be, or not to be, that is the question." There is some of Hamlet's hesitation in Hetfield's narrator. Later in the song, he reflects, "No one but me can save myself, but it's too late." To even consider the possibility of being saved indicates that there is still some last bit of hope. He is right that he will have to save himself, but he is wrong that no one else can help to save him. Again, this is typical of the all-or-nothing thinking of the depressed mind. The narrator realizes the truth that he must take action to save his own life, but he falsely concludes that no one else can help. His conclusion that "it's too late" is also mistaken. The fact that he is still thinking about it shows that there is still time. He can change his mind. The narrator's hesitation and uncertainty become clearer in the next line, "Now I can't think, think why I should even try." The narrator's inability to think clearly should give him pause and encourage him to delay action. The line, though, transforms from a general inability to think into a specific inability to think of any reason to continue trying. We don't know specifically what range of treatments the narrator has tried. Perhaps there is something new or different that he could try or try again? Even if he has no confidence that any future treatment would work, he could pause at what stops Hamlet, the realization that he does not know "what dreams may come" in the sleep of death. Perhaps death is not a dreamless sleep in which one ceases to be. Perhaps something even worse awaits us in the afterlife if we take our own lives. If that thought crosses the narrator's mind, he does not mention it. He simply notes that "yesterday seems as though it never existed." In other words, he cannot recall a time when he felt differently, when he was not suffering the pain of depression. Of course, he can recall that there was a time in his life when he was not depressed, but he feels oddly detached from those memories, as if they belong to someone else, as if the things he recalls happened to someone else.

Personal identity is bound up with memory, specifically the first-person perspective on our own memories. So to lack connection with what has happened to us in the past is indicative of major problems. A memory that we once felt differently and better is an anchor that provides a sense of stability. With that memory, recovery is a matter of getting back to where one belongs, of coming home, as "Confusion" depicts it. To say that "yesterday seems as though it never existed" is to say that memories now seem like stories of something that happened to someone else that do not give *you* hope or inspire *you* to act. It had already been difficult for the narrator to imagine enduring tomorrow and all the tomorrows that would follow. Now even the yesterdays are unimaginable, and the pain of today makes life unendurable.

As the song concludes, the narrator says, "Death greets me warm." It is a striking image, reversing our usual expectations. We think of death as cold and icy, the bony finger of the Grim Reaper. Yet here death is warm and welcoming. Despite these details, Hetfield purposely leaves a lot out of the song and up to our imagination. The narrator has resolved to kill himself and has taken action. How? By what means? "Fade to Black" is a long suicide note that concludes with death greeting the narrator and the narrator signing off with "Now I will just say goodbye." Death seems to be coming over him slowly and warmly. He has not shot himself or hanged himself. Maybe he swallowed a fatal dose of pills and feels a certain warmth and comfort, a feeling that an end to his suffering is near. No one else matters to him at this point, but it seems like he will not be leaving a messy corpse to be discovered. Perhaps he'll even appear to be at peace when someone discovers his body.

Suicide, by overdose or other means—the song depicts a sad situation. I count myself among the depressed teenagers who took comfort in "Fade to Black," understanding that I was not the only one who'd ever felt that way. I'm sure the song saved lives. Rather than rescue the narrator at the last moment, Hetfield imagines the suicide all the way through and forces us to do likewise. There is nothing to be celebrated in the ending; a person has died and is not coming back. So, as long as the listener has an ounce of hope or fight left in him, he is encouraged to fight on. The song's message isn't that life is miserable and not worth living. Quite the contrary, the message is that life is worth living as long as there is hope that one can remember a yesterday when things were better and imagine a tomorrow when they will be better again. The fighting spirit of Metallica's music appeals to people who suffer and yet maintain the belief that they can take action to make things better. So, in the context of Metallica's larger message, "Fade to Black" becomes a catharsis for suicidal feelings rather than a catalyst to suicide.

If the returning soldier who narrates "Confusion" were to contemplate suicide, his experience would probably be different from that of the narrator of "Fade to Black." The emotional landscape for the narrator of "Confusion" is not despair but a sense of persecution and delusion. As he describes it, "Crossfire ricochets inside me / Trapped in a memory forever." He is no longer on the battlefield, but he experiences his civilian life as if the perils of a war zone were still his reality. As he says, "All sanity is but a memory." Unlike the narrator of "Fade to Black," the narrator of "Confusion" can at least recall a time when he was happy, sane, at home in his own head. However, he cannot seem to imagine a tomorrow in which he will have returned to the sanity he remembers from before combat.

If the narrator of "Confusion" were to contemplate suicide, his ruminations might resemble those in "Just a Bullet Away" from the EP *Beyond Magnetic*. The narrator flirts with the idea of killing himself with his own gun. In fact, the flirtation is no mere idea. Night after night he takes the gun out and puts it in his mouth: "Death upon the fingertips / Frigid metal touches lips." It's as if he only feels alive at the point of taking his own life. Paradoxically, only these moments of nearly taking his life relieve his pain: "Caressing death again / Becomes the heroin / Forbidden medicine." The song tells a story of decline as the narrator speaks of "a hope so paper thin." In truth, the relief he gets from bringing the gun to his lips is starting to fade: "Even the promise of danger has gone dull / Staring down the barrel of a .45." He is not the first to play this game, saving his life temporarily by taking action to end it and then withdrawing. The song's narrator observes that "All reflections look the same / In the shine of the midnight revolver." The lines suggest that everyone who plays this game has the identical look of desperation. It is not yourself whom you see in the cloudy mirror of the gun metal. Rather you see the image of despair. We are not privy to the narrator's specific motivation for wanting to kill himself. The closest we get is an accusation directed at an unnamed person: "'Cause you lied / Yes you lied." Who lied? What was the lie about? We do not know, but if we imagine the narrator of "Confusion" as speaking those lines, we might suppose he is directing his accusation at the military recruiters, commanding officers, doctors, and others who misled him in the beginning or promised false hope in the end. Easily we can imagine the narrator of "Confusion" committing suicide with the final lines of "Just a Bullet Away": "Just a bullet away from leavin' you / Just a bullet away / Stop the voices in my head." After all, that is what the narrator of "Confusion" wanted to stop, the voices in his head. The "you" he wanted to leave was himself, or what had become of himself, "trapped in a memory forever."

Drug addiction is another suicidal path that we could readily imagine for a returning soldier like the narrator of "Confusion." Indeed, it's one of the detours that Odysseus and his men take on their return home from the Trojan War, becoming lotus-eaters trapped in a narcotic haze. Another song from *Beyond Magnetic* portrays this form of subtle suicide. Inspired by the sad fate of Layne Staley from Alice in Chains, Hetfield penned the lyrics to "Rebel of Babylon," which depicts the pathetic existence, self-aggrandizement, and death of a drug addict. Rather than shoot himself like the narrator of "Just a Bullet Away," the character in "Rebel of Babylon" flirts with death differently. For the narrator of "Just a Bullet Away," sticking the barrel of the gun in his mouth delivers a high: "Caressing death again / Becomes the heroin." For the Rebel of Babylon, it is not metaphorical heroin but the literal drug that provides his escape from the pain of life. No single act of shooting up is an act of suicide for the Rebel, but the pattern of behavior constitutes subtle suicide in which death is welcomed, even though it is not strictly planned. Rebel is slowly killing himself by living the way he does, and he knows it. In effect, he is playing Russian roulette. Any injection could bring an overdose and death. As the song's narrator chides poetically, "Go take your poison ink / Sign life away / Then take your dirty spoon / And dig your grave." The misery of addiction, with its prolonged and uncertain road to death, makes a bullet seem like a sane alternative. Perhaps there is something of Hamlet's indecision in Rebel's dance with death. "To be, or not to be"—that is the question that Rebel does not even ask himself. Instead the narrator asks, "Rebel is it hard to leave / What makes you stay?" In other words, why not just kill yourself and get it over with?

Rebel's actions and attitude seem to provide an answer: he thinks that it is cool to die young from addiction. The world will see him as a sensitive soul who gave all that he could. The narrator mockingly imagines Rebel jabbing himself with the needle and saying, "Kill me one more time / Stigmata / Kill me one more time / Neo martyr." The Rebel sees the track marks on his arms as stigmata, the wounds of the crucified Christ. He believes he's martyring himself, dying for a cause. But what is the cause? In his warped vision he must see himself as sacrificing his life for his art, believing that only by feeling the pain of life so deeply can he create art. The pain, though, must be treated with the

THE MEANING OF METALLICA

drugs, which themselves eventually bring more pain than relief. He is thus spiraling towards death, towards martyrdom. It is a losing cause, and he knows it. Rebel is past the point of thinking that he can live successfully in the throes of his addiction, but his inflamed ego makes him more than a mere martyr. The narrator sees through Rebel's grandiosity: "Renegade fights the fight / That no one wins / He claims a crown of thorns / To pierce the skin." The Rebel thinks of himself in Christ-like terms. He is persecuted and misunderstood. The needles he injects are like the crown of thorns, meant to mock him but (in Rebel's mind) a sign of his true glory. Still, why does he do it? Why is he killing himself? The narrator has the answer when he describes Rebel's deluded state of mind: he thinks he will achieve immortality by living on in fame. As the narrator tells the story, "He climbs his crucifix / And waits for dawn / Thinks they'll remember him / After he's gone." Getting on the cross, which he does willingly, does not bring immediate death. Unlike Jesus, Rebel is not forced to get on the cross, but like Jesus he takes a while to die. There is no swift end, as there would be with a bullet to the head. Still, Rebel finds resolve to continue on his path, telling himself, "Gonna die young / Gonna live forever." Ultimately, the character is not really a rebel but a fool. No one truly achieves immortality by living on in the memories of future generations. What lives on is only some image or thought of the deceased person, and besides, it's only temporary. Even Homer and Shakespeare will one day be forgotten.

"Rebel of Babylon" is a cautionary tale. As the Whore of Babylon from the book of Revelation is associated with the Antichrist, who will mislead humanity, so the Rebel of Babylon has misled himself and, by his example, tempts others down the path to an early death. Instead of celebrating the likes of Jimi

Hendrix, Jim Morrison, and Layne Staley, we should learn from their mistakes. Dying young from addiction is not the way to go. In writing "Rebel of Babylon" Hetfield embodies an alternative, continued creativity in a life of fulfilling sobriety. The same message comes from another cautionary tale, "Moth into Flame" from *Hardwired . . . to Self-Destruct*, a song inspired by Amy Winehouse. Indeed, the album's title reflects the addict's apparent inability to avoid self-sabotage.

The song title "Moth into Flame" suggests a degree of freedom. We can imagine the moth having a choice, and so we are perplexed at why it would fly into the fire. Telling the story of a "pop queen," the song is another case of subtle suicide; the diva drinks a heady brew of narcotics and fame to tame her dissatisfaction with herself. As Hetfield describes it, she will "overdose on shame and insecurity." Unlike Rebel, the "pop queen" doesn't see the end coming. In fact, she thinks she's still on the way up, not the way out: "You're falling, but you think you're flying high." The "pop queen" seems to think that the life of excess is required for artistic success, and she deludes herself into thinking that she is unique in her creativity despite being a cliché in her indulgent behavior. Really, she is just acting out the same sad pattern that the public has seen many times before. As Hetfield sings, "Same rise and fall / Who cares at all? / Seduced by fame / A moth into the flame / Addicted to the / Fame." As with Rebel, the "pop queen" was not just addicted to drugs, she was hooked on fame. But whereas Rebel craved fame that would live on after his death, the "pop queen" was most interested in keeping her name in the tabloid headlines with outrageous, drug-fueled antics. The immediate aftermath of tragic death boosts notoriety, as "the vultures feast around you still." The paparazzi take pictures, the newspapers run stories, and trend-chasing fans buy music.

Soon enough, though, the "pop queen" is forgotten. "Now you're thrown away." Her story, her life, is disposable entertainment. People have seen it before, and they will see it again. When it comes to the real person who suffered and died, "who cares at all?" The implicit answer to the rhetorical question is no one. Some rock and roll saints live on in infamy for a time, but most don't last long. All the more so, regular people who follow the tempting path of the pop queen and the Rebel to self-destruction are soon forgotten.

There is nothing glamorous about dying from addiction, but what about dying for romantic love? Shakespeare's *Romeo and Juliet* famously tells the story of the star-crossed teenage lovers who tragically commit suicide when each mistakenly believes the other is dead. Life without the beloved seems unthinkable and unlivable. Such is the madness of romantic love that it would cut us down in our prime rather than be denied. In this light, *Romeo and Juliet* is also a cautionary tale. Beware the insane things that romantic love will tempt you to do. You will soon enough regret them if, unlike Romeo and Juliet, you live long enough. We can hear the voices in Meatloaf's "Paradise by the Dashboard Light," who ruefully look back on the youthful promises that bound them together, singing, "It was long ago and it was far away / And it was so much better that it is today." Indeed, the male voice wishes for death, singing, "I'm praying for the end of time / It's all that I can do / Praying for the end of time / So I can end my time with you." Only death will free him from his living nightmare, but he's not prepared to do it by his own hands. The Grim Reaper will have to take him. Speaking of which, in "(Don't Fear) The Reaper," Blue Öyster Cult tells the story of a suicide pact between lovers. The song does not promote or endorse suicide, but it does imagine that "Romeo and Juliet / Are together in eternity." Of course the characters have been immortalized in literature, but do people live on after earthly death? No one knows, and it would be foolish to end one's life prematurely based on that hope.

In "Now That We're Dead," Metallica satirizes Romeo and Juliet's suicide with the lines "Now that we're dead, my dear / We can be together / Now that we're dead, my dear / We can live, we can live forever." Imagine the silliness of saying how great it is to be dead—now we can finally be together and live forever. Yes, it can be noble to accept death when it has become truly inevitable. As Hetfield sings, "When reaper calls / May it be / That we walk straight and right." However, there is ambiguity in the song. It does not seem like death is inevitable for the narrator and his beloved when he says, "When we're seduced / Then may it be / That we not deviate our cause." Rather than nobly accepting inevitable death, it sounds more like they are foolishly falling for a trap. They are seduced by one another, by the intoxication of romantic love, and by the promise of an afterlife. Seduction rarely results in a good outcome, preying on our emotional nature and overriding our rational judgment. Curiously, though, the song undercuts this reading with the final lines "Return to ashes, shed this skin / Beyond the black, we rise again / We shall live forever." The theme of rising again recurs in Hetfield's lyrics, and here it seems earnest in projecting a post-mortem existence. So maybe Blue Öyster Cult was right; maybe "Romeo and Juliet / Are together in eternity" after all.

Rising again from death is also an important theme in "Trapped Under Ice" from *Ride the Lightning*. The song's title at first invites images of falling through a crack in a frozen lake and coming up under the ice, unable to break through. The moments of terror would be excruciating, but probably brief before you sank into unconsciousness and hypothermia. As we listen to the lyrics, however, we learn that Hetfield is envisioning an enduring state that occurs as a result of cryonics. The ice from the title is not some pond or lake but the frozen state of a dead body, preserved through cryonics for a future time when it can be revived and cured of whatever killed it. Some super-wealthy people, including Walt Disney, are rumored to have been preserved in such cryonic states. The song imagines the terrible scenario in which a person frozen in the cryonic state somehow comes back to life without anyone else realizing it. "From deep sleep I have broken away / No one knows, no one hears what I say." The narrator, probably stored in a freezer, is fully conscious but unable to move or communicate: "Freezing / Can't move at all / Screaming / Can't hear my call." The awful fictional situation resembles a rare but real-life situation in which a patient under anesthesia is awake and feels the pain of surgery but appears unconscious and is unable to communicate. As terrible as the fate of the patient is, at least the surgery comes to an end. By contrast, the cryonic survivor in the song sees no end in sight to his suffering, describing it as "hell, forevermore." Indeed, Dante's *Inferno* depicts the lowest level of hell filled not with hot flames but with frozen ice. If there is a hell, maybe that is what it is like, an iced-in solitary confinement in which "woken up, I'm still locked in this shell." Without a hint of irony, the cryonic victim says, "I am dying to live," and to no avail cries out, "I'm trapped under ice." Having woken from a state of death, he wants to break free and truly live. But, if the narrator is indeed alive and awake in his cryonic state, it would be reasonable to wish for death instead. Really, if no one is going to hear his silent screams, then death would be a desirable alternative—a return to the sleep from which he woke. Indeed, Hetfield imagines this desire for death in a similar scenario in another song, "One," with which the next chapter begins.

# CHAPTER 5

# WAR

## *The Bell Tolls for One Disposable Hero*

"One" from the album . . . *And Justice for All* envisions the terrible scenario in which a soldier has been badly disabled by battle: "Landmine has taken my sight / Taken my speech / Taken my hearing / Taken my arms / Taken my legs / Taken my soul / Left me with life in hell." Unable to see, hear, or speak, the decerebrated soldier appears to be in a persistent vegetative state. With help, his heart beats and his lungs breathe, but his brain does not think—or so it is wrongly presumed. The soldier is actually fully conscious but deprived of all sensory input; his own thoughts are all the company he has. As the soldier describes it, "Now the world is gone, I'm just one." It is the ultimate form of solitary confinement, a torture we would not wish on our worst enemies. The soldier has difficulty telling if he is awake or asleep: "Can't tell if this is true or dream." Considering the terrible circumstances of his waking life, dreams must be desirable. Perhaps he dreams that his body is fully functioning. In his dreams he can see, hear, speak, and move. To wake from his dreams is to find himself in the recurrent nightmare of reality: "Back in the womb it's much too real / In pumps life that I must feel." Horrified, he would like to cry out, but he cannot. "Deep down inside I feel to scream / This terrible silence stops me." A scream can free us from a nightmare by waking us, but no such escape is there for the soldier. He is unable to scream, unable to change his state.

Influenced by Venom's "Buried Alive," the song begins with moody, atmospheric sounds. For the first line of the song, Hetfield laments, "I can't remember anything." Amnesia is a common result of traumatic injuries, but gradually the soldier reconstructs his memories and realizes his situation. As he describes it, "Fed through the tube that sticks in me / Just like a wartime novelty / Tied to machines that make me be." He is an oddity, something that should not be, a freak kept alive by machines. There is no real value in being this kind of "wartime novelty." He is not like a returning soldier with a missing limb and an inspiring story. Instead, he is a useless remnant, discarded to a dark room where "Now that the war is through with me / I'm waking up, I cannot see / That there is not much left of me / Nothing is real but pain now."

The pain is what others fail to perceive. From their perspective he appears unable to think and unable to feel pain. His sincere wish is that the medical personnel would "cut this life off from me." Hamlet's question gives him no pause. If only they would disconnect the tubes, he could cease to be. Alas, his own efforts are fruitless. "Hold my breath as I wish for death," but he knows that won't work. He cannot kill himself, even though he wants to. The martial beat of the drums and the staccato delivery of the lyrics impart urgency and inevitability to the picture they paint: "Darkness / Imprisoning me / All that I see / Absolute horror / I cannot live / I cannot die / Trapped in myself / Body my holding cell." All he can do is wait. And no matter how long it takes, it will certainly feel like forever. He has no fear of what may await him after death, confident that it will not be worse than what he is living through.

The idea for the song "One" goes back to the *Master of Puppets* era, with Hetfield musing about what it would be like for someone to be conscious but unable to communicate. Later, Metallica's manager, Cliff Burnstein, suggested that they watch the World War I movie *Johnny Got His Gun* (1971), clips from which were interspersed with performance footage to make Metallica's first video. Released during the Vietnam War, *Johnny Got His Gun* packed a potent message concerning the futility of military conflicts in which people lose their lives for reasons they do not always understand or endorse. Metallica's "One" was released in 1988, a time of relative peace prior to the first Gulf War, yet the anti-war theme of the film and the song resonates with Metallica's earlier songs.

Taking inspiration from chapter 27 of Ernest Hemingway's *For Whom the Bell Tolls*, Metallica's song of the same name depicts the nobility of soldiers while questioning the point of their enterprise. Metallica's "For Whom the Bell Tolls" from *Ride the Lightning* (1984) begins with the sound of a bell and Cliff Burton's otherworldly bass, ominously signaling the emotional landscape of men on the battlefield at dawn. "Make his fight on the hill in the early day / Constant chill deep inside / Shouting gun, on they run through the endless grey." The cause seems noble, and perhaps it is. But how much thought went into decisions that would result in great costs for small gain? "On they fight, for they are right, yes, but who's to say? / For a hill, men would kill. Why? They do not know." Perhaps nothing could be clearer to the soldiers than that they are on the side of justice, but for a moment there is a pause from the narrator's perspective with the question "who's to say?" Is there room for doubt? Is this battle really necessary? Was there no other way to settle the conflict? Now the five soldiers are poised to kill and be killed for the sake of a hill. Is it worth it? Perhaps. Maybe the hill has enough strategic value in a battle that is so crucial to the goal of winning a justified war, that the loss of life is a price worth paying. Then again, maybe not, especially when one's own death seems inevitable.

Hemingway took the title of his book from a poem by John Donne with the immortal lines "Any man's death diminishes me, / Because I am involved in mankind, / And therefore never send to know for whom the bell tolls; / It tolls for thee." The poem's first line is "No man is an island." Donne's lovely sentiment rings true on a certain level. With the death of a friend or family member, we lose a part of ourselves. Few of us, however, experience the death of a stranger as a loss of part of ourselves. Donne calls us to a greater sense of community in our common humanity. Rather than take the attitude of "better him than me," Donne wants me to see the other person as part of myself. It is a tall order, made more difficult by our tendency to see death as something that happens to other people. We recognize in abstract terms that someday we will die, yet we often do not accept the concrete reality of our own mortality, imagining in some way that we are an exception to the rule. Confrontation with death can shake us out of our denial and delusion. We come to realize that the bell tolls for us, not just in the metaphorical sense of losing part of ourselves with the death of others, but in the literal sense that we ourselves will die. Dodging a bullet can thus fill us with resolve and appreciation, a commitment to live life to its fullest. On the battlefield, though, the next bullet may have our name on it.

In "For Whom the Bell Tolls," "shattered goal fills his soul with a ruthless cry." Victory, defense of the hill, fades from view. Hetfield depicts the inevitability of the soldier's death in a desperate situation, instructing him to "Take a look to the sky just before you die / It's the last time he will." We can imagine the soldier realizing that this battle will be his last. There will be no survival or surrender. At a moment like that, time can stand still, as the sight of the sky takes on heightened beauty and relevance for its finality. Yet, he wrestles with death. "Stranger now are his eyes to this mystery." Death is close, but it remains foreign and paradoxical as "he hears the silence so loud." According to the chorus, "For whom the bell tolls / Time marches on." The bell tolls for thee in the literal sense that you personally will lose your life, and with each moment that passes death creeps closer, whether you are on the battlefield or in bed. However, the constant march of time will cease when the unimaginable occurs, when you die, when your consciousness is snuffed out. Perhaps, though, in the confrontation with death the soldier glimpses the truth and understands the reality in a way that eludes most of us. "Now they see what will be, blinded eyes to see." Perhaps in that final moment the blinders that block our eyes fall away and death makes sense.

"For Whom the Bell Tolls" not only challenges us to face the specter of death but makes us question the purpose of war. The individual soldier seems lost in the fray, diminished and devalued. Still, the song leaves open the possibility that because the fight may be justified, the sacrifice may be worth it. "Disposable Heroes" from *Master of Puppets* leaves far less room for interpretation along those lines. Again, written and released during a time of relative peace, the song is much stronger than its predecessor in its anti-war message. Though no historical war is invoked as the setting, one cannot help but think of Vietnam. By 1986, the year of the song's release, public opinion had settled firmly in the view that the Vietnam War was a terrible mistake. A generation of young men had been used as pawns in a senseless game. Many lost their lives, and many more bore scars both visible and invisible. Consider that, for example, the anti-war film *Platoon*, set in Vietnam, was released later the same year. The cover of *Master of Puppets* (1986) depicts a military cemetery with crosses as far as the eye can see. A helmet and dog tags hang from crosses in the front. Barely visible puppet strings reach down from hands in the ominous sky above, connecting "Disposable Heroes" with the title track and the theme of control and manipulation that runs through the album.

"Disposable Heroes" begins with the voice of an omniscient narrator. As if ruefully noting that he has run out of toys, puppets, to play with, he laments, "Bodies fill the fields I see, hungry heroes end / No one to play soldier now, no one to pretend." The fields he sees are cemetery fields, but the song will take us on a tour of the battlefields that led to the cemetery fields. It has been a game of "pretend" in which truth is put aside for other purposes. From the perspective of the malevolent narrator, the human life of the individual soldier is of value only to the extent that it advances the game of war. The narrator is not so much an individual commander as he is a symbolic War Pig watching the action safe from a distance. Describing the process by which human pawns are made and disposed of, the narrator sneers, "Soldier boy, made of clay / Now an empty shell / Twenty-one, only son / But he served us well / Bred to kill, not to care / Do just as we say / Finished here / Greetings, Death / He's yours to take away." The age of 21 is actually on the edge of too old for effective military indoctrination, but "twenty-one" rhymes with "only son" and so it fits the song. At the age of 18 or 19, young men are even more malleable, even more "made of clay." The description of the soldier boy as an empty shell could be taken a couple of ways, and perhaps both are implied. In one sense, the soldier is emptied of his previous thoughts and inclinations and filled with new ones by his military training. As a clay vessel, he is emptied of his old contents and reshaped to fit new demands, broken down and poured out, only to be rebuilt and refilled according to military specifications. In short, he has been "Bred to kill, not to care / Do just as we say." There can be no hesitation on the battlefield; the order to kill cannot be second guessed; the human faces of the enemy cannot inspire care. The soldier boy has been shaped to follow orders, not question commands.

The second sense of being an empty shell may refer to the end of his life on the battlefield, at which point much has leaked out and little is left to give. When the narration switches to the soldier's point of view later in the song, we get a sense of the empty shell's point of view. But as far as the malevolent narrator is concerned, the soldier is a useless, spent unit by the end. Yes, he's young and someone's only son, but there's no need to get sentimental about it. "Finished here / Greetings, Death / He's yours to take away." Giving a sense of the low regard in which he holds the young recruit, the narrator barks, "Back to the front / You will do what I say, when I say / Back to the front / You will die when I say, you must die." The soldier boy is indeed disposable from the narrator's point of view. The soldiers in "For Whom the Bell Tolls" die for a hill, but they may see it as part of a bigger plan. The soldier boy in "Disposable Heroes" is simply told to follow orders without questioning, including the order to die in a dubious battle. This "only son" may be regarded as a "hero" by the people back home, but that's not the way his commanding officer, the narrator, sees him.

To his credit, the malevolent narrator is honest with himself, even if he is not honest with those he commands. He does not kid himself into thinking that he loves and respects his men. Quite the contrary, with contempt he growls, "Back to the front / You coward / You servant / You blind man." The soldier boy has been taught that the essence of bravery is to charge into battle without question or hesitation, but the narrator mocks him as a coward. Courage, the narrator knows, is not the absence of fear. Rather, it is the proper use of reason to govern fear. In this case, the soldier boy is actually cowardly for not giving voice to his fear and questioning the value of what he is being asked to do—sacrifice his life. The malevolent narrator is a master, and by contrast he labels the soldier boy a "servant." The direct address of "you servant" makes clear that it is no compliment. He is thought of not as a faithful or dedicated servant but rather as a slave. Worse still, it is his own fault that he is a slave. He could have resisted and broken free of his slavery, but he is a "blind man"—not literally, of course. He could not be blamed if he were literally without sight, but he can be blamed for allowing himself to be blinded by his military indoctrination. We listeners do not blame him harshly, of course, because we understand that he lost his ability to see little by little over the course of his training.

As the narration switches to the soldier, we realize that he has some awareness of what has been done to him. Perhaps it would be better if he didn't, though. Maybe, in this case, ignorance is bliss. As if echoing the jeers of his commander, the soldier sings of "Running blind through killing fields, bred to kill them all / Victim of what said should be / A servant 'til I fall." He realizes that he has been "bred" to be blind and unquestioning, and as a result he is a "victim" and a "servant." Nonetheless, he has no sense that he can do otherwise. His training, his programming, has him "running blind" towards his own grave. He has become inured to the sounds of battle. With a casual tone, the soldier boy notes, "Barking of machine gun fire / does nothing to me now / Sounding of the clock that ticks, get used to it somehow." What clock? Is it the ticking of a time bomb? Perhaps. Metaphorically, though, it may be the clock that counts down to his own extinction, the realization that time is running out for him with every minute that passes. Military glory is among the mistakes he makes, thinking that it is worth chasing, falling in with the "glory seeker trends" and the foolish belief that "more a man, more stripes you wear." The indoctrination and the contagion of groupthink have him pursuing pointless distinctions. Even realizing the error of his ways, he cannot help being swept up in the jingoistic charge for glory. As he notes, "Bodies fill the fields I see / The slaughter never ends." Curiously, he doesn't say whose bodies, those of his comrades or those of the enemy. Presumably both. If victory were decisive, with his side untouched, his attitude would likely be different. Instead, there is nothing but carnage, and telling one side from the other is impossible. It is a "slaughter," as if the soldiers on both sides were caught up in the mechanical process that leads animals to their end, with all the blood and guts that entails.

The blinders fall from the soldier boy's eyes as he asks, "Why, am I dying?" He is not injured, lying in a hospital bed, when he asks that question. No, he is healthy on the battlefield. In a sense it's true that we're all dying from the moment that we are born, but this is not his insight. Rather, he realizes that the likely outcome of his service will be his death. It seems only a matter of time. He doesn't know exactly how much time he has; he doesn't know which bullet will have his name on it. He can hear the clock ticking. The bell will toll for him. A voice intrudes: "Kill, have no fear." His training and his commander's words echo in his head, attempting to drown out the existential question. He can override his fear with dishonesty: "Lie, live off lying." The fabric of falsehood is for a moment apparent, but he has made it this far by believing the lies told to him from above and from within. The enemy hates you and is out to destroy your nation's way of life. The enemy is less than human and deserves to die. These are the kinds of lies he has lived off, while knowing that the truth is more subtle, more nuanced. As if realizing it for the first time, the soldier declares, "Hell, hell is here." It's a cliché to say "war is hell," so much so that it diminishes the power of the words and insight. The Vikings imagined war as leading to paradise, as the Valkyries would take the fallen heroes to Valhalla. A warrior who was unlucky enough to die an ignoble death somewhere safe and far from battle might be relegated to hell—not the terrible place of Christian imagination but a bland place with none of the excitement that a warrior craves. The soldier boy of the song has rightly come to reject promises of reward and glory in death, and he also seems to reject fear of punishment in the life to come, realizing that if there is a place of punishment and torture it is here, now.

Crying out in anger and despair, he declares, "I was born for dying." It may be the first time that he has fully realized the existential truth that he has been dying since the moment he was born, that the end is inevitable and probably pointless. Some people are able to hide from that truth for their whole lives, acknowledging only in principle that all people die and that someday they will die too. Facing the truth forces a person to take stock in how they have been living. Unfortunately for our soldier, when he looks back over his life he is not pleased. Long before he entered the military, forces were at work. Parents, priests, and teachers had their ideas and put them into practice. "Life planned out before my birth, nothing could I say / Had no chance to see myself, molded day by day." Listening to the song, we have no idea how strict and controlling his upbringing really was, but from his current perspective he thinks it left him no wiggle room, no freedom. Certainly, though, his parents didn't hope or plan for him to die in battle at a young age. Like all parents they probably had dreams for their child and rules that he had to follow. No matter how strict their upbringing, though, most children rebel and shake off authority at some point. This is not easy.

The soldier boy of "Disposable Heroes" is 21 when we meet him, but he was probably 18 when he was drafted and began his military programming. If he is fighting in Vietnam, then boys his age dodged the draft and protested the war. We cannot hold him fully responsible for the situation in which he finds himself, but there were alternatives. Unfortunately, he was raised to follow authority, and the result is that he will die without the chance to live a full life. In a moment of clarity, he says, "Looking back I realize, nothing have I done." Of course, his life has had its moments and maybe even accomplishments, but none of them have been authentically self-chosen. He has done what he has been told to do, trusting that others know better and believing that if he plays by their rules he will be rewarded. The stark reality of that lie now stares him in the face as he concludes, "Left to die with only friend / Alone I clench my gun." No one has really been a friend to him, not in the deep sense of telling him the truth and making him face it.

The song's story does not specify the details of his final mission. Is he literally alone at this point, cut off from his comrades in arms? Or has he simply come to realize the truth, that he has been alone all along, even in the midst of other people? The ambiguity allows us to picture both. Likewise, we are left to wonder who his "only friend" is, himself or his gun? In a way, he has not even been a friend to himself, trusting others to mold him and tell him what to do. But he is at least a friend to himself in this last moment of self-honesty. On the other hand, we could read the gun as being his only friend. The final line is ambiguous. Perhaps the gun has become his safety blanket. Or maybe he is getting ready to take action. On this interpretation, is he gripping his rifle tight, getting ready to go out in a blaze of glory, cut down by the enemy? Or does he "clench" the gun to pull its trigger on himself? The latter seems less likely, but it is suggestive of a line of thought. He doesn't need to commit suicide with his own gun. All he needs to do is expose himself to enemy fire. The result will be the same: he will be one more body to fill the field of battle and then one more body to fill the cemetery field. Either way, the commander's attitude is the same: "Finished here / Greetings, death / He's yours to take away." The soldier boy was indeed disposable, even if not really a hero in the commander's eyes. There will be time for ceremonial mourning at some point, but not now. The song ends with the malevolent commander repeatedly barking at others, "Back to the front."

Two other Metallica songs, "Fight Fire with Fire" and "Blackened," echo the anti-war theme, though they do not focus on the plight of an individual soldier. "Fight Fire with Fire" from *Ride the Lightning* warns of nuclear devastation as the absurd outcome of seeking vengeance and trying to equalize the score.

The song begins with the line "Do unto others as they've done to you." Isn't that what Jesus said? No, he said, "Do unto others as you would have them do unto you." Big difference. Jesus's message was to turn the other cheek and to treat others as you would like to be treated. That advice, however, is seldom followed in the realm of international politics, where taking an eye for an eye is standard policy. Alas, as Gandhi observed, that policy will leave the whole world blind. Even worse than worldwide blindness, modern weapons can "blow the universe into nothingness" with the result that "nuclear warfare shall lay us to rest." This is no holier-than-thou judgment from Hetfield. Released in 1984, as the cold war raged on, "Fight Fire with Fire" simply reflected the angst we all felt that "Time is like a fuse, short and burning fast / Armageddon's here, like said in the past." The rapid repetition of the title phrase "Fight Fire with Fire" to close the song suggests the tit-for-tat matching and escalation that could lead to the dreaded end. Somehow that has not happened, at least not yet.

Although "Blackened" from . . . *And Justice for All* (1988) is most often interpreted as a song about environmental abuse, certain lines—"winter it will send" and "millions of our years / In minutes disappears"—suggest themes of nuclear fear, echoing "Fight Fire with Fire." Indeed, "Fire / To begin whipping dance of the dead" readily suggests helpless hordes fleeing the fallout of a nuclear winter. Again, no solution is proposed, but that is not the purpose of the song. Instead it is a wake-up call. Past wars have done unspeakable damage to millions of individuals, but nuclear war could lead to "cancellation . . . human race."

# CHAPTER 6

# JUSTICE

## *Don't Tread on America for Revenge*

F ar from weepy or whiny, Metallica's anti-war songs are muscular and powerful in their sound and message. Nonetheless, a song from The Black Album seemed out of place when it was released in 1991. "Don't Tread on Me" strikes the listener as a celebration of the warrior and maybe even a glorification of war with its military, marching music. Did Hetfield do an about-face? No, it's not that simple. Part of the problem is that some critics have mistakenly read the song as an endorsement of the Gulf War and the American invasion of Iraq. In fact, though, the song was written and recorded before the war and the invasion, even though the album came out just after those events. The actual inspiration for the song was the Culpeper Flag, which hung in the recording studio. Designed in 1775 in the Revolutionary War spirit, the flag captures the American ethos and pride. Metallica's previous album, . . . *And Justice for All,* had been a negative reflection on certain elements of American government: greed, corruption, and censorship. For Hetfield, "Don't

Tread on Me" was a tribute to the American spirit that persists despite the negative elements. The Culpeper Flag has since become associated with the Tea Party movement and other right-wing elements in American politics, but we need to remember that the song far preceded those associations.

"Don't Tread on Me" reflects the fact that you can be anti-war without being a complete pacifist who opposes all wars under all circumstances. "One" drew on World War I imagery from *Johnny Got His Gun*, a film that implicitly aimed its critique at the Vietnam War. Indeed, Hetfield may have been caught up in the wave of condemnation of Vietnam during the 1980s. Practically no one now thinks that Vietnam was a good or worthwhile war, and the legacy of World War I is doubtful. Couldn't the conflict have been avoided? Was American involvement necessary? By contrast, few, if any, would argue against American involvement in World War II. Notably, though, America stayed out of the conflict until we were attacked by the Japanese at Pearl Harbor. The Culpeper Flag reflects all these sentiments.

Benjamin Franklin and others considered the rattlesnake that adorns the Culpeper Flag a symbol of America. You don't want to mess with a rattlesnake. You don't want to step on it or even get too near it. Respect its rights and its territory. If you get too close, you'll notice a warning sound: "Once you provoke her, rattling of her tail." When you hear that, it's time to back off. The rattlesnake does not come to your territory looking for trouble, and it expects the same courtesy in return, even firing a warning shot in the form of its signature sound. The rattlesnake does not start fights, but it does finish them, as the lyrics suggest: "Never begins it, never, but once engaged . . . / Never surrenders, showing the fangs of rage." With the Declaration of Independence, the newly formed American nation said to the world, leave us alone and we'll leave you alone. Yes, America would have peaceful trading relations with all countries but no military interventions. The British did not agree to those terms, and they suffered the consequences. Against all odds, the ragtag colonial army defeated and expelled the redcoats. For those who do not heed the warning of the rattle, well then, "So be it / Settle the score / Touch me again for the words that you'll hear evermore / Don't tread on me."

Sadly, America has not always lived up to the non-interventionist military policy symbolized by the Culpeper Flag. Nonetheless, the ideal has been, as Teddy Roosevelt put it, to walk softly and carry a big stick, or as Hetfield sings, "To secure peace is to prepare for war." The flag pays tribute to the snake as the symbol of America standing sentinel: "Quick is the blue tongue, forked as lighting strike / Shining with brightness, always on surveillance / The eyes, they never close, emblem of vigilance." Unfortunately, preparedness breeds temptation. It's easy to forget that the purpose of an army and an arsenal is to avoid using them if at all possible. Both before and after the song's release, America fell prey to the temptation to tread on those who had not tread on us.

The force of the flag and the "Don't tread on me" motto must be directed not just at other nations but at the American government itself. The album cover for . . . *And Justice for All* features Lady Justice bound by ropes (puppet strings?) with her scales tilted and overflowing with cash. The title track bemoans the corruption of the legal system: "Halls of justice painted green / Money talking." Although inspired by watching CNN, Hetfield references no current events. As a result, the song is not dated. It rings as true today as it did then.

Censorship is the other major justice issue addressed by . . . *And Justice for All*. The hearings for the Parents Music

Resource Center (PMRC) were still fresh in memory, as was the case of Jello Biafra of the Dead Kennedys, who was nearly ruined over prosecution for an insert (*Penis Landscape*) that accompanied the album *Frankenchrist*. Again, the songs on . . . *And Justice for All* do not reference current events, despite being inspired by them. In fact, "The Shortest Straw" draws on imagery that could describe the communist Red Scare of the 1950s: "Witchhunt riding through / Shortest straw / The shortest straw has been pulled for you." Nonetheless, the "witchhunt" description fits the concerns of the 1980s about explicit lyrics and supposedly lewd art, and of course the description continues to capture different sets of concerns about free speech and expression today, as it likely will in the future.

"Eye of the Beholder" is more explicit in its critique: "Independence limited / Freedom of choice / Choice is made for you, my friend / Freedom of speech / Speech is words that they will bend / Freedom with their exception." The final line captures the crux of the problem: if freedom of speech has exceptions, then it is not really freedom. The First Amendment to the US Constitution guarantees more. Of course, there are constitutionally recognized limitations. As Oliver Wendell Holmes Jr. famously said, you can't shout "fire" in a crowded theater. In other words, you cannot incite a riot or cause harm to others through false or negligent speech. But those limitations are rather slight and do not bear on artistic expression. No one is harmed by supposedly vulgar or obscene art. Plenty of people may be offended, but there is a big difference between being harmed and being offended. Clearly, artists have the right to be offensive.

Speaking to and for artists and fans, Hetfield sings, "Do you fear what I fear? / Living properly / Truths to you are lies to me." The realm of art and speculative ideas does not deal with the settled facts of science. The song's title refers to the cliché that beauty is in the eye of the beholder. What you value and consider true may be lies to me—certainly it is wrong to dictate standards of taste and decency. You don't have to like what I like or listen to what I listen to. You just need to leave me alone. Society flourishes when people are allowed to live experimentally and express themselves in contrasting ways. Waving the flag for freedom of expression and the variety it brings, Hetfield sings, "Do you choose what I choose? / More alternatives / Energy derives from both the plus and negative / Do you need what I need? / Boundaries overthrown / Look inside, to each his own."

"Eye of the Beholder" is not anti-American. Nothing could be more American than to use freedom of speech to protest limitations on freedom of speech in an attempt to right the wrong. Indeed, the song strikes a patriotic note when Hetfield intones, "I hunger after independence, lengthen freedom's ring." The sentiment is not to subvert America, but to call America to be its best self. Fittingly, the album takes its title from a phrase known to every American from the Pledge of Allegiance. The word "liberty" is missing from the title of the album, however, implying that it is missing from the system. There is no justice without liberty. After all, it is the "sweet land of liberty" in which we sing, "Let freedom ring."

In contrast to the white album cover for . . . *And Justice for All*, a plain black cover shields the eponymous *Metallica*, also known as The Black Album. Whereas the previous album features an image of secular sacrilege, Lady Justice with cash overflowing from her scales, The Black Album features an image of militant patriotism, the rattlesnake from the Culpeper Flag. It is tempting to see the images and messages as opposing or contradictory, but they are not. Rather they are the two parts of a single whole, the yin and yang of the American spirit. In fact, the message of . . . *And Justice for All* is don't tread on me—don't limit my freedom of speech and don't corrupt my justice system. I won't stand idly by—I will strike back.

The word that joins the protest of . . . *And Justice for All* to the protest of "Don't Tread on Me" is "liberty." As noted, "liberty" is the word ominously missing from the album's title phrase, and the concept is invoked in Hetfield's wish to "lengthen freedom's ring." Indeed, he says, "I hunger after independence." The American colonies achieved independence by defeating and expelling the British, but the struggle ever since has been to secure independence for individual Americans. "Don't Tread on Me" captures the spirit of the American Revolution when Hetfield sings, "Liberty or death, what we so proudly hail." The lyric references Patrick Henry's famous speech in which he implored Virginia to supply troops for the Revolution, concluding, "Give me liberty or give me death." The sentiment continues to speak to Americans and people around the world: it is better to die fighting for freedom than to live in chains. America is the land of opportunity because it promises liberty, individual freedom. That promise must be continually renewed, warning those who would compromise it in the name of some other ideal that the rattlesnake's "eyes, they never close, emblem of vigilance."

One line from "Don't Tread on Me" remains troubling, however. A certain intolerance can be heard in "love it or leave it." Surely, those aren't the only two possibilities. The third possibility is to reform it, and this is what Hetfield was calling for with . . . *And Justice for All*. Rather than hear the line as spoken to someone with whom Hetfield disagrees, we can hear it as spoken to himself. Despite the justified complaints about corruption and censorship, Hetfield did not stop loving

America. In fact, the protest songs were written out of love as well as anger. It just takes some reflection on his part and our part to realize it. We must find a way to love America despite its faults, to get our country to live up to its highest ideals. To love America is not to accept it as it is, but to want it to grow and improve. America is not a finished product but a developing process. Certainly we should not tell anyone other than ourselves to love it or leave it. And we should recognize that others love America even if the changes they want are not the same as the changes we want. Progress is not always straightforward, but it results from the competition of ideas, freedom of expression, and freedom to live as one chooses so long as one does not harm another person.

In "Eye of the Beholder" Hetfield sings, "Do you trust what I trust? / Me, myself and I / Penetrate the smoke screen, I see through the selfish lie." A rugged individualism and ethos of self-reliance characterizes American culture and informs Metallica's music. Nonetheless, a sense of community is important, especially for the outcast. In this spirit, the imagery of war was employed on Metallica's debut album. Belonging, a sense of community, matters, and it makes life more fun and worthwhile. The young Metallica issues a call to arms for like-minded individuals to join together in a "metal militia." There are no uniforms, just "your leathers and your spikes." The causes are not noble, just doing a little senseless destruction while spreading the gospel of heavy metal: "Oh, through the mist and the madness / We're trying to get the message to you."

With songs including "Metal Militia," "Phantom Lord," "No Remorse," "Seek and Destroy," and "The Four Horsemen," *Kill 'Em All* is a pure celebration of revenge and warrior virtues. Using the imagery of the warrior to represent adolescent, existential crisis and rebellion, the message is clear: life is war, "war without end." The struggle is not to be taken literally, of course. *Kill 'Em All* was unparalleled in its appeal to angry, alienated, suburban, white teenage males (like I was) for whom life was a struggle despite dwelling in comfortable conditions with no real war to fight. Rather than simply accept that life sucks and fade to black, we took up the fight against whoever, whatever. As we saw it, war is hell, and life itself is war.

Unlike later albums, *Kill 'Em All* employs a lot of fantasy imagery, the kind that quickly becomes cliché if not handled properly. A war makes no sense without an enemy, and nothing unites a group like a common enemy. So the fantasy imagery works well for its vagueness and symbolic power. With a little imagination we can envision fighting on the side of the Phantom Lord: "Hear the cry of war / Louder than before / With his sword in hand / To control the land / Crushing metal strikes / On this frightening night / Fall onto your knees / For the Phantom Lord." Who is the Phantom Lord fighting? Who would oppose him? Anyone who would look down on metal and its culture—and in 1983 that was almost everyone: parents, teachers, preppies, jocks, you name it. If you're alienated and angry in the early 1980s, metal is your music and you are bound together with like-minded fans as comrades in arms. You can imagine an ultimate victory: "The leather armies have prevailed / The Phantom Lord has never failed."

Drawing inspiration from the book of Revelation, Hetfield pictures the Four Horsemen who signal the end of the world. The music to the song "The Four Horsemen," originally written by Dave Mustaine, was changed only slightly when he was kicked out of the band. But Hetfield completely rewrote the lyrics and altered the title from "The Mechanix." Mustaine's music has a galloping sound that perfectly fits Hetfield's lyrics. Rather than just witness the riders, we are instructed to join them: "Lock up your wife and children now / It's time to wield the blade." In Hetfield's retelling, the Four Horsemen are time, famine, pestilence, and death. There is no Jesus on a white horse and no hope for eternal salvation. It is simply payback time: "So gather 'round young warriors now / And saddle up your steeds / Killing scores with demon swords / Now is the death of doers of wrong / Swing the judgement hammer down / Safely inside armor blood guts and sweat." The fantasy of revenge feeds the narrative and appeals to the alienated teenage listener. He who is ridiculed, persecuted, and powerless will someday rule the land. The imagery is violent and unforgiving, as in these lines from "No Remorse": "Blood feeds the war machine / As it eats its way across the land / We don't need to feel the sorrow / No remorse is the one command." The soldier in battle cannot afford to hesitate or freeze with second thoughts or regrets, but this is something more. "No mercy for what we're doing / No thought to even what we've done / We don't need to feel the sorrow / No remorse for the helpless one / War without end." The song glorifies the lack of feeling for the pathetic victims. It is a fantasy, suitable to play out in a video game or a heavy metal song, and it can be cathartic. The imagined victory is cleansing and lets one return to the real world more at ease.

In the real world, remorse and restraint are required. Consider that "Don't Tread on Me" is not exactly about revenge but about protecting your rights and your property. The song is about responding to an actual threat with appropriate force so as to make the attacker regret his action and think twice about repeating his mistake. By contrast, "No Remorse" and "The Four Horsemen" are about meting out punishment for perceived wrongs in the past, not responding to immediate threats in the present. The *Kill 'Em All* mentality is not about taking an eye for an eye, a tooth for a tooth. It goes well beyond that, taking revenge in excess of what is warranted. Again, this can be a potent and cathartic fantasy, but it is no way to actually live.

"Fight Fire with Fire" from the next album presented the more mature view that taking revenge can lead to a cycle that ends with everyone dead. Hetfield borrowed the phrase "Ride the Lightning" from another poet, Stephen King. Fittingly, the title track depicts a man awaiting his execution in the electric chair. The song's narrator admits he's "guilty as charged" but still insists that "damn it, it ain't right." Hetfield personally did not oppose the death penalty, and he said that the song was just meant to depict the horror a man experiences going to the chair. But the narrator complains, "Who made you god to say, / 'I'll take your life from you'?" So we might wonder, what good comes from the man's execution? If it simply satisfies a desire for revenge, then maybe we should rethink the law.

"Here Comes Revenge" from *Hardwired . . . to Self-Destruct* takes stock in the insidious desire to seek vengeance. The song was inspired by the story of a young woman, a Metallica fan killed by a drunk driver. Her parents subsequently came to Metallica concerts as a way of connecting with something their daughter loved. The song is Hetfield's attempt to put himself in their shoes; he would want revenge on the killer. "You ask forgiveness, I give you sweet revenge / I return this nightmare, I will find you / Sleepless, cloaked in despair, I'm behind you." The narrator realizes, however, that seeking vengeance in this way would not be satisfying. Rather, it would be poisoning. As he plays out the scenario and sees where it leads, he realizes that "Revenge, is killing me." That is the sad truth of the situation.

Revenge will not set the balance right. Instead, it will further disturb those who have already been harmed. The song's narrator shifts to the voice of Revenge itself, saying, "Man has made me oh so strong / Blurring lines of right and wrong / Far too late for frail amends / Now it's come to sweet revenge." The powerful desire for revenge can be intoxicating, doing away with ordinary concerns for proportion, justice, and balance. And it is a desire that feeds upon itself and leaves us feeling, at best, momentarily satisfied. The young fan's parents were right not to seek vigilante justice against the person who killed their daughter. Far better is to leave that to the criminal justice system, imperfect though it is.

As the saying goes, living well is the best revenge. This practical wisdom can provide comfort for those who have been wronged in the breakup of a romantic relationship, but it holds some truth for those who have been wronged in any circumstances. If the parents of the young Metallica fan allowed themselves to be consumed by the need to punish the drunk driver, they would only be adding to the damage done. Instead, they cultivated their love for their daughter by embracing her love for Metallica. In that sense, they lived well.

## CHAPTER 7

# FREEDOM

*Wherever the Unforgiven Wolf Roams*

Metallica means freedom, and "Wherever I May Roam" is a declaration of individual independence, a freedom manifesto. The song starts with sitar, evoking visions of the Far East, but this is an American tale, in which the narrator abruptly announces, "And the road becomes my bride." A striking beginning, it leaves us wondering who he is leaving and where he is going. We need not worry that this will be a cringeworthy song of self-indulgence in which a rock star complains about how tough it is to travel from town to town. Instead, the narrator is an ordinary person who pledges himself to the road life, embraces it as his wife. He thus becomes extraordinary and inspires us to aspire to be like him. It is no easy path ahead, but in the spirit of American adventure from Mark Twain's *Adventures of Huckleberry Finn* to Jack Kerouac's *On the Road*, there will be much to learn.

We already know that the narrator will not be held back by anyone, but then we learn that he will not be weighed down by anything: "I have stripped [myself] of all but pride." His provisions are minimal, and his pride is an asset. Rhymes bring us back to the bride as the narrator tells us, "So in her I do confide / And she keeps me satisfied." We the listeners will not hear the narrator's secrets. But he tells them to the road, and that is enough. As the metaphor plays out, the road is the lover who takes care of him emotionally and physically, "gives me all I need."

The second verse lets us know that this will not be a magical journey to a perfect place. The narrator depicts difficult conditions: ". . . And with dust in throat I crave." So we are not to imagine the air-conditioned luxury of a sedan. He may be traveling by car, by motorcycle, or by foot. But whatever his mode of transportation, conditions are not comfortable. Nonetheless, he relishes the road because of the freedom it delivers. He takes what he needs and discards the rest. Hetfield sings, "Only knowledge will I save." As we'll see, this is a journey of discovery, and it is self-knowledge that the narrator seeks above all else. He already knows what he is not; he already knows what he rejects — the life he left.

Switching to the second person, the narrator mocks those who are stuck where he was: "To the game you stay a slave." He sees most people as pawns in a game that they do not control. They may think they are in charge, buying a house and climbing the corporate ladder, but they are really slaves. Without even realizing it, they serve the interests of more powerful people by trying to satisfy desires they did not create or choose for themselves. Every once in a long while, though, someone refuses to play the game and leaves. The response is predictable. People do not praise and admire the rebel. Instead, they mock and label him, as the narrator knows: "Rover, wanderer / Nomad, vagabond / Call me what you will." The narrator has been labeled all his life, and these particular labels, like "wanderer," are not compliments. They can be transformed, though. As J.R.R. Tolkien told us, "Not all who wander are lost."

Indeed, Hetfield's wanderer has embraced the freedom of his chosen life. No one tells him where to go or when: "I'll take my time anywhere." He faces no restrictions on his words and thoughts. Polite society no longer dictates what he can and cannot say: "Free to speak my mind anywhere." Listeners can't help but admire and desire such freedom, as we bite our tongues ten times a day and regret the results when we don't. Of course, this freedom comes at a price. The narrator has traded the comfort and certainty of domestic dwelling for a life of nomadic wandering. To those he left behind, his bare-bones existence may look like hell. But in addition to the *freedom from* constraints he now enjoys, the narrator also has *freedom to* look at the world as he chooses. As he says, "I'll redefine anywhere." He has the freedom and ability to create something unexpected out of his circumstances.

In John Milton's epic poem *Paradise Lost*, Satan finds himself cast out of heaven. Rather than bemoan his fate, Satan reasons, "The mind is its own place, and in it self / Can make a Heav'n of Hell, a Hell of Heav'n." Hetfield's narrator is no Satan, but he is saying something similar in fewer words. His mind is free to redefine what a good and successful life is. Beyond that, he is free to redefine himself. Other people can label him however they want, but he is free to reject those labels and reconceive himself. And he will. In first-person narration, Hetfield sings, "Anywhere I roam / Where I lay my head is home." It is the journey, not the destination, that matters. Anywhere will do. Home is redefined. Home is not where the heart is, or anything silly or sweet like that. Home is where I am, wherever I am.

**THE MEANING OF METALLICA**

A powerful realization leads the narrator to declare, ". . . And the earth becomes my throne." Penniless, he is king of the world, servant to no one. It is a grandiose image but fitting to his freedom, not just *freedom from* societal constraints but *freedom to* create and make the world and himself as he desires. Civilized society delivers certainty in the form of ready meals, prepackaged conversations, and warm beds. It is this comfort and certainty for which we trade our freedom. The narrator has struck a different bargain, welcoming the challenges and adversity of the road. As he tells us, "I adapt to the unknown." In the absence of domestic certainty, he has become an improvisational actor who readily makes the most of what is thrown at him. More than that, he relishes the challenge because of the improvement it catalyzes. The verse continues, "Under wandering stars I've grown." We can picture him traveling at night, camping under the stars. No pain, no gain; growth comes only as a result of pushing past personal boundaries. He is stronger, not just physically but mentally and emotionally. Before hitting the road, he had been dependent and fragile, but now he is independent and firm.

The next line is paradoxical: "By myself but not alone." How can you be by yourself but not alone? The lyric could be a reference to a divine guide, whether God or something else. That interpretation, though, is undercut by the final line of the verse, "I ask no one," which suggests that the narrator is not praying to anyone for anything. So we are pushed to look for a different interpretation. You can be by yourself even when you are in a crowd or among a group. You can, for example, come by yourself to a party and be among friends while remaining your own person and going home by yourself at the end of the night. For contrast, consider George Thorogood's line "When I drink alone / I prefer to be by myself." There are two ways to drink alone: in the company of others at a bar or party, or by yourself at home alone. A person could be alone and by himself, like a hermit who shuns contact with other people. But Hetfield's narrator is not that way. Rather, he is by himself as a one-man team, interacting with other people but counting on no one. Sometimes alone but never lonely, he thus embodies the rugged individualism that is so much a part of the American spirit.

In case we have any doubt about the narrator's personal connections, the next verse begins, ". . . And my ties are severed clean." We might have been tempted to imagine that he had some mixed feelings, that he missed at least some of the people he left behind. If he had any of those feelings, he has eliminated opportunities to indulge them. Likewise, he has not kept connections with anyone he worked for. Like the invading army that burned its ships at the shore, he has no option to retreat, no plan B. This allows him to move forward with conviction and without hesitation. In the first verse the narrator has "stripped of all but pride." So he has taken nothing of material value with him. Pride is what civilized society was trying to take away from him, perhaps telling him that it is a sin. He has rejected that hypocritical message. After all, the people who discouraged pride nonetheless took excessive pride in their possessions and accomplishments.

Poetically, the narrator realizes, "The less I have, the more I gain." By freeing himself from material possessions, he has opened himself to much more. Unlike the people he left behind, he does not have to slave away at a traditional job to make money to buy stuff that no one really needs. So what does he "gain"? The answer was given earlier when he told us, "Only knowledge will I save." His hands are no longer grasping and holding on to mere things. His hands are open, and so is his mind. The journey is one of self-knowledge and self-discovery. He takes the road less traveled, the one where he is a king, servant to no one. As he puts it, "Off the beaten path I reign." The narrator has blazed his own trail, and he lives by his own rules. Does he transcend all circumstances? Certainly not. He has no magical abilities to change the world. Rather, he has the ability to make the most of any situation, because he will not be defined by it. As he tells us, "I'll never mind anywhere." Why? Because "I'll take my find anywhere." His "find," his discovery, is that he owns his mind and defines himself. As a result, he will only grow in the power of self-knowledge, tested by the ever-changing conditions he meets.

Hetfield's narrator has set out on a journey of self-discovery that will only end when he is in the grave, or perhaps not even then. Envisioning his death, he tells us: "Carved upon my stone / My body lie, but still I roam." This is a curious passage because of its ambiguity. It seems to suggest that his soul will live on after his death and continue the journey. That religious sentiment would fit with interpreting the earlier line "By myself but not alone" as referring to God as his constant companion. The traditional view of heaven, though, is not a place of roaming but a place of rest. So another religious way of taking the passage is hinted at by the Indian sitar that starts the song. Perhaps his soul will continue to wander after his death because it will be reincarnated, as Hindus and Buddhists believe. Maybe he will come back as a wolf. Finally, though, we might take the wording less literally to mean that no one can kill the narrator's spirit. In fact, this is true. He lives on in song, in spirit, inspiring us. We identify with the narrator as we listen to the song, and we aspire to be more like him. We probably won't leave everything behind and set out on the road, but hopefully we will follow his lead by shunning convention, seeking knowledge, growing from pain, and defining ourselves. Hetfield himself is inspiring in these ways, though he too falls short of the ideals set by his narrator.

"Of Wolf and Man" features a narrator who is a kindred spirit to the narrator of "Wherever I May Roam." In fact, like the previous narrator, he can be found "*roaming* the land while you sleep." Hetfield, an avid hunter, clearly drew inspiration from his love of nature in writing "Of Wolf and Man." It would have been easy to turn a song like this into a werewolf tale like Ozzy Osbourne's "Bark at the Moon." Of course, Metallica's song flirts with lycanthropy in the lyric "shape shift," but the overriding theme is one of naturally discovering authentic wildness.

In *Civilization and Its Discontents*, Sigmund Freud argued that humanity pays a price for the calmness and order of civilization. We warp ourselves by repressing our natural sexual desires and aggressive tendencies, which find other ways to express themselves, often coming out sideways and causing neuroses. Hetfield's narrator would agree. But rather than prescribe Freudian psychoanalysis, Hetfield's narrator has a more natural cure.

We don't need to spend years on a psychiatrist's couch. Instead, we need to embrace our animal nature. Near the end of the song, the narrator says, "I feel a change / Back to a better day / Hair stands on the back of my neck / In wildness is the preservation of the world / So seek the wolf in thyself." The oracular imperative "know thyself" becomes "seek the wolf in thyself." Without a foundation of self-knowledge, no lasting structures can be built. Civilization tries to make us into domestic sheep. Whether we are following the good shepherd into religious conformity or the great leader into political conformity, the outcome is the same. We lose ourselves and become something we are not meant to be. No wonder we are miserable.

We can hear Hetfield the outdoorsman in the lyrics "I hunt / Therefore I am," but there is more to it than an endorsement of predation and conservation, "harvest the land." The narrator is not simply practicing good stewardship by thinning the deer herd. He depicts "taking of the fallen lamb." The lamb, like the sheep, is a domesticated animal, but one with even more religious resonance. The lamb has fallen and is to be devoured. This narrator will serve no gods and no masters. Freud thought religion was a human creation exploited by the powerful to keep people in their lowly place. So he would approve of devouring the lamb.

Hetfield's narrator does not identify with a domesticated herd animal but with a wild pack animal. For the most part, though, he seems to reject the pack, making the lone wolf his ideal. No doubt, this draws on the experience of hunters setting out together into the woods—"Company we keep"—but then staking solitary stands where they wait for their quarry. The abilities deadened by civilization can be reawakened and heightened by hunting or just spending time in nature. With "nose to the wind" we become attuned to what we would otherwise miss. Indeed, we become more alive, with "all senses clean," perceiving much that we filter out in the artificial environments of our day-to-day lives. This feeling of being at home in nature is "earth's gift" and it takes us "back to the meaning of life." We are not meant to be domestic herd creatures. We are wild animals. We are wolves. We are predators.

Civilization wants us to believe that we are something different, but as the proverb says, "Man is a wolf to man." We dominate and prey upon one another. The cooperation that civilization makes possible brings comfort and security, though only at the price of denying what we are. Hetfield's lyric "call of the wild" refers to Jack London's famous novel of that name, about a dog who rediscovers his wild nature when he is taken north to Alaska to work on a sled team. We can identify with the dog, knowing that we repress an important part of us to operate in polite society. Many of us are fine with the trade-off, but as Freud's title phrase suggests, some of us, like Hetfield's narrator, are discontent. What, though, leads us to be discontent? Why would someone want to hit the road and roam or even self-redefine as a wolf? "The Unforgiven" provides an answer.

The narrator of "The Unforgiven" is not a hero, not really, because he dies "regretfully." (As is revealed towards the end of the song, the third-person narrator and the first-person narrator are the same individual. So let's simply refer to "the narrator.") The introductory music is somber, but the first words are hopeful: "New blood joins this earth." We celebrate the birth of a child—it always seems miraculous. The child in the song is described as "new blood," a positive image. Blood is the stuff of life, and when we speak, for example, of adding "new blood" to a business or organization, we express hope for renewal and revival; we anticipate fresh ideas from different perspectives. In the song, the new blood joins "this earth," and that sounds particularly promising, almost as if the child were coming from above to renew humanity. Such hopes are dashed, though, by the next line: "And quickly he's subdued." Whatever fresh perspective or new ideas the child might bring will not be welcomed. Rather than be set free to create, the child will be hemmed in. Yes, children can be feisty and irrepressible, but in this case, "Through constant pained disgrace / The young boy learns their rules." Alas, the institutions of society are ready for him. They don't merely tell him what their rules are, they enforce them, inflicting pain and disgrace on the boy, breaking his spirit.

Things only get worse: "With time, the child draws in." This "new blood," whose childlike sense of wonder wanted to express itself for all the world to hear, is silenced by force, "this whipping boy done wrong." They make an example of him, telling him what to do, how to act, what to say. Beyond that, he is "deprived of all his thoughts." They even tell him what to think, inflicting guilt upon him for mere thoughts. Retaining some sense of resistance, though, "the young man struggles on and on." He knows they have crossed the line with their demands for his conformity. They may be able to dictate his words and actions, but he makes "A vow unto his own / That never from this day / His will they'll take away." He will not let them censor his mind; he will struggle to keep the fight alive in his thoughts even if not in his actions.

The trajectory of a life has taken shape across a few short lines, from baby, to child, to whipping boy, to young man. The chorus reveals that the young man's vow has left him sorrowful, because he retains his hopes and dreams, despite his inability to act on them. Hetfield sings, "What I've felt / What I've known / Never shined through in what I've shown / Never be / Never see / Won't see what might have been." The narrator has not lived up to his potential because he has not expressed his thoughts and feelings. Instead, he has lived within an institution, the soft prison of society and its demands. The narrator is sensitive and could probably produce the kind of poetry found in the song itself. Unfortunately, though, he'll never get to be or see "what might have been." Looking back on our lives, we commonly regret things we have done, but more often we regret things we should have done. We are saddened at the thought of dreams, goals, and ideals not pursued. As the poet John Greenleaf Whittier rendered this insight, "For of all sad words of tongue and pen / The saddest are these, 'It might have been!'" The words can be pathetic when voiced by someone who wants credit for what they could have done, but they are most truly sad when they are spoken with a sense of defeat, as by the narrator of "The Unforgiven."

The chorus continues, "What I've felt / What I've known / Never shined through in what I've shown / Never free / Never me / So I dub thee Unforgiven." The narrator claims that he was "never free," but his own words belie this claim. Yes, it is true that his circumstances have been terribly limiting. From birth he has been taught the rules he must follow, and he has been punished severely for any transgressions. He has not been ideally free; he has not been given permission to develop his own unique self and let it shine through in his words and actions. Yet, he tells himself a lie when he describes himself as "never free." It would not have been easy, but it would have been possible to break free, as the narrator of "Wherever I May Roam" did. The fact that the "Unforgiven" narrator retained free will within the context of his upbringing and subsequent life in society means that he must take responsibility for his inaction.

In addition to claiming that he was "never free," the narrator says he was "never me." Again, he overstates the case. The truth is that he did not become the person he wanted to be, his true and authentic self. Instead, he lived a life of conformity, pleasing others and living by their standards. Yet, within his own mind he remained aware of this, and admitting it brings him pain. He was himself in his thoughts, but he did not express them. His thoughts and self-conception "Never shined through in what I've shown." Mixed with his sadness, the narrator feels anger, and he looks for someone to blame. At this point he does not target himself. Rather, he turns outward, saying, "So I dub thee

Unforgiven." The narrator resents those who have put labels on him and coerced him to conform to their expectations—of a son, student, church member, citizen, and so on. He finds what they did unforgivable, or at least the only power he is able to summon is the resentful reaction of labeling them unforgiven and refusing in his heart to forgive them. (Of course, they are not seeking his forgiveness, but it might be better for his own sake to offer them forgiveness in his heart, rather than to live with the festering resentment.)

The song continues, "They dedicate their lives / To running all of his / He tries to please them all / This bitter man he is." Living through the mistreatment, he perceives the agents of authority in his life as spending all their time and energy running his life. He long ago stopped resisting them. Instead, he tries to please them all, but there are so many agents of authority that pleasing them all is an overwhelming task. We can easily imagine that some of them have contradictory demands and that some of them have unspoken rules that keep him guessing. The predictable result is that he is bitter, resentful. Who wouldn't be? It's juvenile, though, to think that other people are only interested in running your life and telling you what to do. It can certainly look that way to a child or adolescent, but an adult should know better. The truth is that agents of authority have an interest in seeing you conform in certain ways and follow certain rules, but they have other interests of their own. So here we get a sense that although the character's bitterness is understandable, it results from an exaggerated perception of his situation.

Unfortunately, he does not outgrow it. As the narrator tells us, "Throughout his life the same." Things don't change, not in any relevant sense. New agents of authority and societal expectations may replace old ones, but he is still yoked to the responsibility of pleasing other people and meeting their demands. A different person might have accepted this lot in life long ago and maybe even cheerfully made peace with it. The suburbs seem populated with people who are happy to don the clothes of conformity, take the train to work, and drive the minivan to church. The narrator is not one of them, though he lives among them, blending in but feeling frustrated. All through his life, "He's battled constantly / This fight he cannot win." The battle is largely internal. He has to fight with himself to conform to their rules and expectations and yet retain his own identity and integrity. We can imagine that occasionally he transgresses the rules. Other people can glimpse his anger and frustration, his desire for a different kind of life. Long ago, though, he gave up the dream of making that different kind of life a reality. All that remains is the knowledge of "what might have been." We can imagine that the wrinkles and lines on his face tell a story of resignation: "A tired man they see no longer cares." It's not quite true that he doesn't care anymore. Rather, he looks like a man who has been beaten by the world and who has no fight left in him. He still cares, though, in the sense that he wishes things had been different.

All that is left for him to do is die. No one expects or demands anything else of him. "The old man then prepares / To die regretfully." He will not die in peace, however. Yes, he may be surrounded by family and the trappings of success, but he is full of regrets. He knows that he has not been true to himself; he knows that he could have resisted, could have broken the invisible chains of society. We are left to wonder how he is preparing to die. Is he sick on his deathbed, looking back over his life? Or is he planning an act of rebellion to end his life? Suicide, after all, would violate the rules of the game he has been coerced into playing. It seems unlikely that he would summon the will to break the rules at the end, especially since he still blames others for the choices he made. The song ends with, "You labeled me / I'll label you / So I dub thee Unforgiven." What is most important to the narrator is revenge in the form of labeling others and withholding forgiveness. It is a sad ending, but perhaps it's not really the ending. The narrator tells us, "That old man here is me." Although he has spoken in both the first person and the third person, it is all one person, one point of view, and a living point of view at that. Perhaps, though, the narrator is expressing himself as a man in his 20s, looking back at his life thus far and imagining where it may go. Certainly, Hetfield wrote the lyrics in his 20s without the perspective of having lived a full life. Unlike the narrator, Hetfield himself had broken many of the chains of conformity that this upbringing laid upon him, but his emotional scars had not fully healed.

The narrator of "The Unforgiven" is emotionally complex and vulnerable. On the one hand, he is bitter and resentful like the narrator of "Dyers Eve," but on the other hand, he is sad and regretful like the narrator of "Low Man's Lyric." Thus "The Unforgiven" serves as a warning, cautioning us about the life-sucking conformity that society so often demands. Without providing detailed specifics, the song manages to make a general and universal point. As the poet e.e. cummings put it, "To be nobody but yourself in a world which is doing its best, night and day, to make you everybody else—means to fight the hardest battle which any human being can fight; and never stop fighting." Clearly, it is a battle that most people cease fighting at some point whether in childhood, adolescence, or adulthood. The result is carbon-copy people on the one hand, and bitter, resentful people on the other. Hetfield's lyrics in general, and "The Unforgiven" in particular, are a call to action, urging us to avoid those fates and instead become our true and authentic selves. This is not a battle that can be won once and for all. Rather, it is a lifelong struggle. At times we may seem to be winning and at other times we may seem to be losing, but being true to the struggle is what ultimately matters.

Some people are born into supportive environments in which the development of their unique talents is encouraged. It can be its own kind of advantage, however, to be born into circumstances in which encouragement, love, and resources are in short supply. When we awaken to realize how much the deck is stacked against us, we can find greater resolve to fight. Part of the message of "The Unforgiven" is that we must play the cards we are dealt. Complaining that life isn't fair won't get us far. If we don't like the cards we're dealt, then we can change the game. We can refuse to play by the rules of society, and we can reject the goals they set for us. Instead, we can form our own vision of who we want to become and develop our talents and abilities to achieve that goal. In large measure, this is what Hetfield did.

For Hetfield, changing the game of life was complicated by his abnormal upbringing. We are all messed up by our parents. Even the best, most well-meaning and open-minded parents can inadvertently damage us. As the poet Philip Larkin said, "They fuck you up, your mum and dad. / They may not mean to, but they do." Hetfield's own story includes being raised as a Christian Scientist under the domination of a religiously zealous father who abandoned the family in Hetfield's childhood. In "The God That Failed" Hetfield wrote about his experience in a church that made the false promise of healing without modern medicine, mocking "the healing hand held back by the deepened nail." Hetfield reconciled with his father, Virgil, many years later. Voicing his grief in response to his father's suffering and death from cancer, in the song "Until It Sleeps," Hetfield sings, "Where do I take this pain of mine / I run, but it stays right my side." In renewing ties with his father, Hetfield made a musical connection. Virgil was fan of country music, and James developed an interest in the genre. In fact, Metallica recorded a country-rock song for their album *Load*, but the song, "Mama Said," was about Hetfield's mother, not his father. Although Hetfield's mother raised him as well as she could, James's feelings towards her were not infused with gratitude. Hetfield's mother did not protect him from his father's extremism. Instead she put her passivity into him: "You gave me your emptiness / I now take to my grave." Hetfield was not blameless. Who is? "I never asked forgiveness / But what is said is done." His mother died of cancer when Hetfield was 16, with the relationship unfinished. "I need your arms to welcome me / But a cold stone's all I see." Nevertheless, Hetfield can admit to his mother, "A son's heart's owed to mother / But I must find my way." In fact, a person's need to find his own path is captured in the mother's advice, "Son, your life's an open book / Don't close it 'fore it's done." Having made his way in life without his mother, Hetfield can admit to the tombstone, "I'm not all you wished of me" and "I took your love for granted / And all the things you said to me." Ultimately, he can ask her permission to move on: "Let my heart go / Mama, let my heart go / You never let my heart go / So let this heart be still."

Earlier in his career, in "Dyers Eve," on the album . . . *And Justice for All*, Hetfield has nothing but rage for his parents. With its furious pace, the music mimics the tantrum of a child, and there is no ambiguity in the song's beginning: "Dear Mother / Dear Father / What is this hell you have put me through." The theme is universal: controlling parents produce a child who is unfit to deal with the real world as an adult. "Believer / Deceiver

/ Day in, day out, live my life through you." The parents are at the same time believers and deceivers—they are not accused of being flagrant hypocrites. Instead they are accused of bad faith—they are self-deceived about the truth of their views and in turn they deceive the child, leading him into false views of the world. The child resists, but he is given no room to disagree: "Pushed onto me what's wrong or right / Hidden from this thing that they call life." The lyrics have a personal feel as Hetfield sings, "Every thought I'd think you'd disapprove / Curator / Dictator / Always censoring my every move." For a sensitive, artistically inclined child, the oppressive parental regime is unbearable. "Children are seen but are not heard / Tear out everything inspired." As the child prepares to leave the nest, he fears that the parental damage has made him unfit: "You've clipped my wings before I learned to fly." Nonetheless, the child musters the courage to leave home. Or, in Hetfield's case, his home is now empty at age 16, with his mother dead from cancer and his father nowhere to be found. Perhaps bold and roaring loudly with newfound freedom, the child nonetheless suffers the distortion of his upbringing: "Innocence / Torn from me without your shelter / Barred reality / I'm living blindly." He issues an indignant but inspiring resolution to make something of life. "No guarantee, it's life as is / But damn you for not giving me my chance." The inevitable setbacks, however, result in self-doubt and resentment. "I'm in hell without you / Cannot cope without you two / Shocked at the world that I see / Innocent victim please rescue me." The escaped prisoner yearns to return to the comfort of his former misery, but he cannot return to his former ignorance—that has been spoiled. And so there is no rescue. The song concludes on a note of extreme bitterness: "Undying spite I feel for you / Living out this hell you always knew."

The undying spite is understandable, even if unwise, but the last line is puzzling. Did his parents always know the truth on some level, that their religion was a false comfort that constructed a false reality? Were they bullshitting themselves? As Hetfield, the narrator, attempts to live in the world and face reality, he experiences extreme cognitive dissonance as the voices of his parents continue to echo in his head and narrate his life.

Earlier, in the song "Escape" from *Ride the Lightning*, Hetfield strikes a more positive tone about his prospects for liberation from the damage done by his upbringing. Maybe too positive. In fact, the song is Hetfield's least favorite on the album and was not performed live until the band played *Ride the Lightning* in its entirety for the Orion Music + More festival in 2012. "Escape" is certainly the most accessible song on the album, slower with a lighter sound and a catchy chorus. The lyrics are heavy, though, as Hetfield announces his intention "To escape from the true false world / Undamaged destiny." The worldview his parents indoctrinated him with was false, though of course they put it forward as true (and for the most part believed it was true themselves).

The song expresses unbridled optimism in the belief that he can leave the "true false world" behind and fulfill his "undamaged destiny." The choice of words is noteworthy. No one except a damaged person (and who among us is not damaged?) would claim to be undamaged or to have a future that is not damaged or hampered by what has happened in the past. The other notable word, "destiny," is profoundly optimistic. Destiny is the path of someone who sees himself on an upward trajectory. He is not fated to succeed like some chosen one, but his talent and ambition will lead to success. Just try to stop him. The past was awful, but it will not constrain him. The line "no damn chains can hold me to the ground" may suggest he holds the key to unlock his chains. Self-knowledge and determination will free him. Later, more pessimistic songs like "Dyers Eve" will reflect the realization that liberation is not so simple, that progress is not easy or straightforward.

In "Escape" we get the sense that Hetfield is whistling in the dark and trying to convince himself that he is "one with my mind, they just can't see" and that there's "no need to hear things that they say." The phrase "one with my mind" suggests that he experiences no cognitive dissonance, that he has completely freed himself from the voices of his parents in his head—he doesn't even "hear things that they say." The song starts with a denial: "Feel no pain." Really, you're not hurt by anything from your past? Are you impervious to pain in the present? Maybe not, as the narrator admits in the same line, "But my life ain't easy." Why? Well, because "I know I'm my best friend." The first-person singular narration is notable in this song because it breaks with the second-person plural narration from Metallica's first album, *Kill 'Em All*. The first album presented an "us against the world" point of view in songs like "Metal Militia" and "Whiplash."

By the time of the second album, *Ride the Lightning*, Metallica is still hungry and aiming to take over the world, but Hetfield allows himself more room for personal reflection. In "Escape," after noting that he is his own best friend, Hetfield amplifies his claim: "No one cares, but I'm so much stronger." To say that "no one cares" seems extreme, but maybe it is somehow appropriate. He has no family. Hetfield's mother is dead and his father is nowhere to be found—so they don't care. What about his friends? They care about him. He's part of a band, a unit that needs to work together to achieve their goals. They kicked out Dave Mustaine prior to recording the first album because his erratic behavior seemed like a hindrance. Surely, Lars Ulrich cared about Hetfield, but the two had such different upbringings that he likely couldn't care for Hetfield in a deep way. Ulrich's parents were permissive and encouraging. How could he relate to, or truly understand, where Hetfield was coming from? Hetfield could channel his drive and creative energy into the band, but his friends and bandmates didn't really care about the demons that drove him. The song's next line proves prophetic: "I'll fight until the end." There is no one-and-done cleansing or catharsis. Indeed, the theme of a personal fight, a "struggle within," echoes through the rest of Metallica's music and Hetfield's lyrics.

The images of what Hetfield is trying to "Escape" from are instructive: "Can't get caught in the endless circle / Ring of stupidity." Many attempts at escape are fruitless precisely because they do not lead up and out but around and around. One ends up right back where one started. Hetfield calls it a "ring of stupidity." One can fall into a ring of stupidity as Johnny Cash sang of falling into a "ring of fire." There's seemingly no escape. Nor is it love and desire from which Hetfield seeks escape. Quite the contrary, it is force and violation from which he flees. "Rape my mind and destroy my feelings." Knowledge is power for liberation. Employing a visual metaphor for understanding, Hetfield tells his tormentors, "I can see through you" and assures them that he will "Break away from your common fashion / See through your blurry sight." The song concludes with a triumphant rejection of the force that held him in place: "See them try to bring the hammer down." It may have worked in the past, but it will not work now, as the narrator proclaims that "no damn chains can hold me to the ground." The song outros with the line "Life's for my own to live my own way" repeated seven times. If this were really the end of the story it would have been enough to say it once. In truth, self-reflection only gets thornier and more complicated over time with the realization that it is a continual process, not a single victory.

## CHAPTER 8

# EMOTIONAL ISOLATION

## *So Close, but Still Unforgiven*

The struggle to self-define and live independently is noble, but taken too far it can lead to emotional isolation. Romantic love can remedy that, making us feel truly understood and appreciated. Metallica's catalog is light on love songs, but two are noteworthy: "Nothing Else Matters" and "The Unforgiven II." "Nothing Else Matters" was not supposed to be a Metallica song. Hetfield wrote it about his girlfriend, Kristen Martinez, expressing the difficulty of being separated by life on the road, "so close no matter how far." The rest of the band liked the song, though, and so it was included on The Black Album.

As a ballad, "Nothing Else Matters" reached a wider audience while not misrepresenting the band. Lyrically, the song makes sense for Metallica, taking up themes of struggle in a context of romantic love. Bonding with bandmates and fans alleviates the pain of isolation, but to really heal you need to be vulnerable with someone. Hetfield admits and expresses this when he sings, "Never opened myself this way / Life is ours, we live it our way." Buddies, bros, and best friends may hear beer-soaked parts of the truth, but the narrator has never told the whole truth of his story to anyone like this before. The result of opening himself up totally is a union different from what he has ever experienced. He and the woman form a team of two, and they live life on their own terms. They have found in one another what has always been missing in their lives. Hetfield sings, "Trust I seek and I find in you."

When, as happened to Hetfield, family disappoints you at an early age, you fashion yourself a suit of emotional armor that you are reluctant to remove. The weight of the armor makes you want to take it off, though. So you seek someone you can trust. The bliss of falling in love is such that you and your beloved have your own little world "and nothing else matters." The joy of love is that of virtual rebirth: "Every day for us something new / Open mind for a different view." You are willing to try new things and consider new ideas. As importantly, what was old becomes new again when experienced together and seen through the lens of love.

Struggle does not cease, however, just because the narrator has found a person who understands and accepts him. He continues to reject the wider world, but now he has a partner in defying societal expectations and demands. In fact, because of his relationship, he may be hearing new demands and putting up with unsolicited opinions. The naysayers are an anonymous "they" in this song, standing in for all those who would chain us with conformity. Hetfield sings, "Never cared for what they say / Never cared for games they play / Never cared for what they do / Never cared for what they know / And I know." The narrator roundly rejects the common wisdom and petty gossip of the crowd. He has rejected it in the past, and now he rejects it in the context of his romantic relationship. He knows better, and together as a couple they know best.

The lyrics conclude with Hetfield singing, "Forever trusting who we are / No, nothing else matters." The romantic sentiment is touching—it's us against the world. We can count on each other, and we don't need anything else. The reality is not so rosy, of course. Most romantic relationships end, and many end in betrayal. We do not know the details of the romantic relationship that inspired "Nothing Else Matters," but we do know that it ended. Hetfield eventually married someone else, Francesca Tomasi.

With rose-tinted glasses removed six years later, "The Unforgiven II" from *Reload* takes another look at the need for emotional connection in a romantic relationship. It is not clear if the narrator is the same one as in the original song, "The Unforgiven." Evidence that the narrator might be the same person includes the phrase "unforgiven too," which makes most sense if we take him as the same person who labeled others "unforgiven" in the original song.

As "The Unforgiven II" starts, the narrator is with a potential soulmate, and he is prepared for the kind of reciprocal emotional exchange that forms the basis of a loving relationship. Indeed, he puts her first, saying, "Lay beside me, tell me what they've done." The anonymous "they" could be her parents, teachers, ex-boyfriends, anyone. We can fill in the blank with our own imagination and experience. Importantly, the narrator is ready to listen, to hear about the pain his beloved has endured; he is ready to take her side and be her support. He recognizes in her a kindred spirit, wounded by the world, damaged but not beyond repair. In turn he will reveal himself; he will tell her what "they" have done to him. In fact, the anonymous "they" reso-nates with the original song, in which "They dedicate their lives

/ To running all of his." This narrator needs courage. He has been wearing emotional armor, but he is ready to take a risk by removing it and letting her see what is underneath. Like all of us, he is haunted by his past, embarrassed by what has hurt him and what he has let happen to him. He senses, though, that telling her about it will unburden his soul. More than that, he trusts that she will know just what to say in response. Thus he asks her to "speak the words I want to hear, to make my demons run." He has kept his secret shame and hurt in the vault of his heart, waiting to reveal himself to the right person.

Hetfield sings, "The door is locked now but it's opened if you're true." The world is full of false people, the anonymous "they." Worse than people who are obviously cruel and uncaring are those who seem kind and trustworthy but turn out to be callous and deceitful. They are not "true," and they certainly cannot be trusted with the secrets hidden in the vault of the heart. The narrator himself struggles to be true, to be genuine and authentic. The world seems to have no place for such people, so it feels miraculous to meet someone else who shares the struggle. It takes time, though, to trust and identify the other person as "true." Another more basic sense of "true" must be presumed in a romantic relationship, namely that the other person will be faithful. When we leap into love, we trust that the other will not betray us, and the pain of a broken heart is awful when our trust is shattered.

The first verse concludes with the hope and promise that "if you can understand the me, then I can understand the you." To feel misunderstood by the world is the fate of nearly every person. For that reason, we treasure those who get us, who really see who we are, and who love us despite our faults. Family and friends may understand us in this way if we are lucky, but we look most often to spouses and significant others for that kind of deep understanding and acceptance. It's not a bargain that is struck—the "if . . . then" structure of the lyric is not a contract or transaction. It is a pledge. More than that, it is a gamble. The only way to make the pledge is to go all in, to risk your heart. Here the pledge includes the odd phrasing of "the me" and "the you." The most obvious explanation for this phrasing is that the line requires the extra syllables. Hetfield could have sung "a me" and "a you," but that would have been misleading. We don't want someone to understand just "a" version of us, but rather "the" true version of us. Of course, "the me" and "the you" is potentially problematic, because people change. There is no such thing as "the me," and I can't reasonably expect "the you" I fall in love with to remain exactly the same over time. In fact, this may be a clue to the problems that develop as the song unfolds. The second verse, however, continues the us-against-the-world bonding.

The poetic imagery is striking, as Hetfield sings, "Lay beside me, under wicked skies / Through black of day, dark of night, we share this paralyze." Hard times do not disappear just because they are in love. Life has not become unicorns and rainbows. The skies are wicked; the days are black; and the nights are dark. This is not a weather report but rather an emotional landscape. The couple is enduring difficult times, but the cause is unspecified. The anonymous "they" may be to blame, or the couple may be enduring relationship conflicts. Either way, the narrator does not push her away. Rather, he beckons her: "Lay beside me." The couple join together, but their problems are not solved. Instead of describing their embrace as shelter from the storm, the narrator says, "We share this paralyze." The image evokes a vision of the couple as frozen, unable to move or act, implying that the problem is internal to the relationship. After all, if the world outside were the source of distress, they would move together against it. More evidence for internal problems comes in the concluding lines of the verse: "The door cracks open but there's no sun shining through / Black heart scarring darker still, but there's no sun shining through." Presumably they opened the doors to one another as they fell in love, but the doors shut when problems arose. During the paralyzed embrace the door cracks open again in an attempt to heal, but it doesn't work. When the narrator opens the door, all that can be seen is his "black heart scarring darker still." If we take the original song, "The Unforgiven," as evidence, we know clearly why his heart is black. The narrator has been mistreated by a world that doesn't want him to be who he truly is. We can wonder whether he is capable of healing, but romantic love and mutual understanding seemed to be his best chance. Now, though, he is worse than when he started. She has inflicted new scars on his black heart.

Romantic love is a risk, but it is impossible to realize how big the risk is until one experiences the pain of a broken heart. The chorus echoes the original song, "The Unforgiven," with the line "What I've felt, what I've known." If we need confirmation that the narrator is the same for the two songs, this line supplies it. "The Unforgiven" imagines an entire life unfolding, whereas "The Unforgiven II" focuses on a particular episode in which the narrator unsuccessfully seeks refuge in romantic love. The chorus continues, framing the narrator's situation from the beginning of the song: "Turn the pages, turn the stone / Behind the door, should I open it for you?" He has begun to tell her about his life, but he needs to decide whether to make himself vulnerable by opening himself completely.

The song then leads into a variation on the chorus: "What I've felt, what I've known / Sick and tired, I stand alone / Could you be there, 'cause I'm the one who waits for you / Or are you unforgiven, too?" The time period captured by these lyrics seems to be deliberately ambiguous. On the one hand, the lyrics seem to describe the past, in which the narrator was bitter and alone against the world, hoping that he would meet someone who would understand him. In this frame, he pictures himself as waiting for a true love and wondering if this is the woman he has been waiting for. His hope, though, is undercut by the line "Or are you unforgiven, too?" He is wondering if she is just like everyone else, all the other people he has dubbed unforgiven.

On the other hand, the lyrics from this part of the chorus may be understood as speaking of a present situation that is unfolding in a way that spells doom for the relationship. When the narrator says, "Sick and tired, I stand alone," he may be describing a scenario in which he is literally waiting for the woman. She is late or has not come home. He holds out some hope that he is not a fool waiting in vain, but he is enough of a realist to wonder if she is like other people who have hurt him. Thus he faces the possibility that she may need to be placed in the category of "unforgiven" like so many others. The details are left to our imagination, but if the narrator is waiting for her and if the relationship is doomed, the chances are that she has cheated on him. Infidelity is painful, but sometimes couples can reconcile.

Unfortunately, the narrator has been so damaged by his past that he does not cope rationally with the infidelity. Instead, he kills her. The song is subtle, but the details are undeniable once we look at the next verse: "Come beside me, this won't hurt, I swear / She loves me not, she loves me still, but she'll never love again / She lay beside me but she'll be there when I'm gone / Black heart scarring darker still, yes, she'll be there when I'm gone / Yes, she'll be there when I'm gone / Dead sure she'll be there." We can imagine the woman confessing her infidelity—she tells him that it was a mistake and that she still loves him. Instead of reacting with uncontrollable rage, the narrator is cool and calculating in killing her. He asks her to come beside him, an invitation she probably interprets as forgiveness. His plan is cold-blooded, but he promises her it won't hurt. Again, we are left to wonder about the details. Does he choke her? Shoot her? The result is that "she'll never love again"; lying beside him a corpse, "she'll be there when I'm gone / Dead sure she'll be there." The creepy scene expresses no sympathy for the woman. Indeed, the narrator seems capable only of seeing things from his own point of view. She has hurt him, and so his "Black heart [is] scarring darker still."

The chorus recurs with one word changed: "Turn the pages, turn *to* stone." It is no longer a story about a man who is going to turn *the* stone to reveal something and potentially make progress, but rather a man whose heart has hardened *to* stone. The first line of the verse after the chorus initially suggests that the narrator feels remorse: "Lay beside me, tell me what I've done." Of course, she can't literally say anything, but her silent witness should trigger horror in the narrator. It does not—there is no horror and no remorse. Describing the situation, he tells us, "The door is closed, so are your eyes." She may be at rest, but she is not sleeping peacefully beside him. She's dead, and he has killed her. As a result, "the door is closed." If the narrator is not aghast at the loss of life, he should at least be saddened by the loss of possibility. For a time, it seemed that he had found a kindred spirit to whom he could bare his soul. Now that possibility is gone, and it is gone in such a way that it makes future connections unlikely. Even if he escapes the law, he will not find another woman who will understand and accept him now.

Nonetheless, he rejoices, telling us, "But now I see the sun, now I see the sun / Yes, now I see it." Perhaps he feels a sense of euphoria, and it seems to him for the moment that the woman was never part of the solution—she was always part of the problem. He had let himself be deluded into thinking that he could trust another person on the deepest level. That had always been wrong, and he is lucky now to realize it. The truth, the light of the sun that he sees, is that he can only ever trust himself. Of course, he is mistaken. "No man is an island," as the poet John Donne said.

Rather than remorse and regret, the narrator feels triumph and satisfaction. He has taken revenge, and he has solved his problem. He had been vulnerable, seeking connection and opening himself to another person, but he will do that no more. Addressing the corpse, he says, "I take this key / And I bury it in you / Because you're unforgiven, too." He vows never again to unlock the door to his heart. Previously we had heard him wonder if the woman was "unforgiven," but now for the first time we hear him label her as such. She belongs to the large group of people who have hurt him. We must wonder whether there is anyone who wouldn't be unforgiven. Most people never get close enough to the narrator to hurt him, but he seems to have concluded that no one is trustworthy and that anyone who got close enough would hurt him. Humans are fundamentally selfish and rapacious, so the only solution is to look out for yourself first, last, and always. For the moment this makes sense to the narrator, and he probably feels foolish for ever letting down his guard. The listener knows, though, that this philosophy and approach to life will not serve him well.

Curiously, "The Unforgiven II" concludes with an echo of "The Unforgiven" as Hetfield sings, "Never free / Never me." In the original song the narrator blamed others for his inability to become his true self. They restricted his choices and made things difficult for him, but he was not fully honest or accurate when he claimed that he was "never free." After all, there are always choices, even at the point of a gun. "The Unforgiven II" ends with the narrator mistakenly blaming the woman for his lack of freedom and inability to become his genuine self, as the final line says, "'Cause you're unforgiven, too." Even more clearly, he is mistaken in this song. The woman may have betrayed his trust, but he was nevertheless free to act differently. He did not have to kill her. Even if it was beyond him to repair the relationship, he could have said goodbye and moved on. If he was unable to forgive her at the moment, perhaps with time he could have found it in his heart. After all, withholding forgiveness hurts the person who withholds it. The resentment that one feels when one refuses to forgive is a heavy burden to bear. Such resentment and anger can fuel us for a short time (think of Dave Mustaine early in his career with Megadeth), but ultimately such feelings deplete us—he who angers me owns me. It is to our advantage to forgive. This does not mean that we need to become best friends with the people who have wronged us or open ourselves to future mistreatment from them. What it does mean is that the best revenge is living well, and living well involves the forgiveness that allows us to rise above past injuries.

The sad fate of the unforgiving person is emotional isolation. The narrator of, "The Unforgiven III" finally realizes this. The song works well on its own, and it has less in common with the first two "Unforgivens" than they have with each other. Nonetheless, it makes sense to take the teller of, "The Unforgiven III" to be the same as the narrator of the previous tales. As in "The Unforgiven," the narration switches between first person and third person while remaining the same narrator. One problem for interpretation is determining where in the timeline the song would fit. Does it occur after "The Unforgiven II"? If so, how did he get away with the murder? And does he really deserve our sympathy? One way out of this dilemma is to reconceive "The Unforgiven II." Maybe he didn't really kill her. Maybe he fantasized about killing her but just walked away. Maybe that is why he can tell us, "Now I see the sun." Let's proceed with that reinterpretation of "The Unforgiven II." In that light, the narrator would have closed himself off from others emotionally. This does not mean, however, that he would have lived like a hermit. As we'll see, the implicit details of "The Unforgiven III" suggest that he lived an ordinary life for a while.

The narrator has always been sensitive to the pain that others cause him through their demands for conformity and through the way they disappoint him. But the second verse of "The Unforgiven III" has the narrator wondering if he might be at fault: "Was he the one causing pain / With his careless dreaming?" He has always wanted something grand and unique for himself, but perhaps others have come to depend on him to be something mundane and common—maybe a coworker, friend, father, or husband. The details are left to our imagination, but the narrator considers that in his "careless dreaming" for another kind of life he hurts other people who need him to be fully present for them. The verse continues, "Been afraid, always afraid, / Of the things he's feeling." From what we have learned in the previous songs, he has not been afraid of feeling anger and resentment. Those are easy things to feel—and he wears them like badges of honor. We can surmise that he has been afraid of feeling love and attachment. His experience of abuse and betrayal make this understandable, but we know that he must overcome his past if he is ever to live well in the present.

The first verse sets the scene and connects us to the sun the narrator sees at the end of second song in the trilogy. "How could he know this new dawn's light / Would change his life forever?" We get the picture that he has been living an ordinary life, but then he is tempted by an opportunity that reveals itself in his routine: "Set sail to sea, but pulled off course / By the light of golden treasure." The narrator's age is not specified here, but it is easy to imagine him in his late 30s, having reluctantly resigned himself to a humdrum existence with an unfulfilling job. Perhaps he acts out the cliché of a midlife crisis. It dawns on him that "he could just be gone," and so he resolves that "He would just sail on / He'll just sail on." As someone who has always craved freedom, he realizes that nothing stops him from abandoning his home and his responsibilities. The nautical imagery lends grandeur and excitement to the endeavor, but the reality may be as simple as driving his car and deciding to keep going past the place where he works. Maybe the freedom of the road opens up before him and he decides to head for the coast where he will finally pursue his dream of becoming a musician, or artist, or entrepreneur, or whatever. We can fill in the blank with our own unfulfilled dreams and aspirations.

The song does not supply details of the euphoria he must have felt at first, fueled by plans for success and visions of achievement. Instead, the song quickly cuts to a scene of self-doubt in which the narrator is wondering, "How can I be lost, if I've got nowhere to go? / Search for seas of gold, / How come it's got so cold?" The answers to his questions are obvious to the listener and maybe even to the narrator himself on some level. He previously thought of freedom as freedom from responsibilities—freedom from work and family, perhaps. Now he realizes that without a framework of responsibilities his freedom is pointless, directionless. There are no seas of gold—there is no smooth road to success. So he finds himself with literally nowhere to go. He is lost, but there is no map or GPS to give him directions. He is a lost soul, not a lost traveler; he has traded the warmth of communal trudging for the cold of isolated wandering.

The questions continue in the next verse: "How can I be lost? In remembrance I relive / And how can I blame you, / When it's me I can't forgive?" Although he has sailed away from home in an effort to leave his past behind, he has taken along the problem: himself. He "relives" the past in his memory, ruminating on it, resenting it—literally re-sensing (or re-feeling) it. Blaming other people for the life he was forced to live and the lost state in which he finds himself, he begins to see his mistake. He can't forgive himself. But for what does he need to forgive himself? The details are left blank, though they are not difficult to imagine. The narrator has been mistreated and coerced into conformity in various ways since childhood, and so he has a long list of people he resents. He imagines that he could have lived a much more fulfilling life if it weren't for all the people who stood in his way. Now he realizes, though, that he feels something in addition to resentment. He feels guilt for having made excuses for himself by blaming others, and he feels guilt for the way he has mistreated others. He has been emotionally distant from others who love and depend on him, and his "careless dreaming" has always told those people that he would rather be somewhere else, doing something else. At this point in his life, it was foolish to run away from home or "set sail to sea" in pursuit of "golden treasure." He will have happiness only when he makes peace with himself and accepts the truth about himself, that he is an ordinary person who can find the most meaning in a life among other ordinary people who love and depend on him.

Although the answers to his questions are just below the surface of awareness, he does not grasp them. Instead of turning his ship around and heading for home, he persists, and "These days drift on inside a fog / Thick and suffocating / His sinking life, outside it's hell / Inside, intoxicating." He started out with a plan and a destination, but now he can't see what will come next and, as we know, he's "got nowhere to go." In addition to its visual limitations, the fog takes on a tactile dimension—it's "thick" like something you'd cut with a knife, and it's "suffocating" like a smothering pillow or billowing smoke. The fog could also suggest drunkenness. It's easy to imagine that the narrator would attempt to drown his sorrows. In his drunken state he might resurrect his plans from a barstool, only to wake the next morning to the realization that he is going nowhere. Rinse and repeat.

The song continues with the nautical imagery: "his sinking life" depicts a vessel in a desperate situation. From any observer's point of view, the narrator's life is full of suffering and misery—"outside it's hell"—but from the narrator's internal point of view, things are ambiguous. Consider the phrase "inside, intoxicating." On the one hand, "intoxicating" can mean exciting, producing a high or a rush. In boozy grandiosity he may imagine how he will somehow someday soon still find "golden treasure." On the other hand, "intoxicating" can simply mean producing drunkenness and can describe something toxic. He is slowly poisoning himself.

The next verse continues the nautical imagery, though it mixes metaphors. First, the narrator is "run aground. Like his life, / Water much too shallow." Depicted as a captain who did not realize that he had sailed into shallow water, he is stuck when his ship rubs against the bottom. Visually this captures the narrator's situation. The outside observer could see that he was in a precarious place, but blown by the winds of self-deception, the narrator just sailed on. He didn't realize how shallow the water was—he didn't realize how shallow his self-absorbed life was. Then the metaphor shifts, as the narrator is described as "slipping fast, down with his ship." We have just pictured him as stuck in shallow water, and now we are invited to imagine his ship going down. Sinking seems impossible in shallow water, but it is another way to envision the narrator's life—as a sinking ship. The final line of the verse departs from the nautical imagery: "Fading in the shadows." Here we can imagine the narrator as disappearing from the minds and memories of the people he left behind. His failure is not a grand event that will make news and arouse curiosity. He will not burn out, but just fade away.

Having run aground, the narrator finds himself in the ultimate form of isolation. "Now a castaway," he is finally free of the tyranny of other people. In his famous play *No Exit*, Jean-Paul Sartre depicted hell as other people. In this damnation drama there are no devils or pitchforks, just three people, specially selected to drive each other crazy for eternity. There is a lot to agree with in Sartre's vision, but as much as other people bother us, it is worse to be utterly alone. Consider that solitary confinement is the most dreaded punishment in prison, as it takes a toll on one's sanity. In the nautical imagery of "The Unforgiven III" the narrator finally finds himself all alone, "now a castaway." He has not gone down with a sinking ship, but like Robinson Crusoe he has been tossed into a scene of extreme isolation. Hetfield sings, "They've all gone away / They've gone away." All his life, the narrator has sought to escape the tyranny of the anonymous "they"—the people who demand his conformity and crush his spirit. Now he has escaped them, but he finds that "they" were not the only cause of his problems. With no one left to point his finger at, the narrator wails, "Forgive me / Forgive me not / Why can't I forgive me?" There is no easy answer to his question, but at least he finally realizes that he is unforgiven too. He has wronged himself as much or more than anyone else wronged him.

It is never too late to make the most of life. Maybe he can go back home again. Returning would take courage, because there is no guarantee that he would be accepted or forgiven. If the narrator forgives himself, then he can forgive his worst abusers, including those who have not admitted their wrongs. He can offer them forgiveness in his heart even if they would scoff at his words. Whether he returns home or starts fresh somewhere new, hopefully he now realizes that a good life requires other people. He needs to love others with all the risk and vulnerability that involves, because only love can heal his wounds and break the chains of emotional isolation.

# CHAPTER 9

# CONTROL

## *The Struggle All within King Nothing*

The title of the song "The Struggle Within" from The Black Album epitomizes much of Metallica's lyrical content. An inner struggle can be noble. Rather than look outward to blame another person for the state of your life, you look within and take personal responsibility. However, "The Struggle Within" does not glorify the war we wage within our brains. Rather, the song mocks the useless tendency to beat ourselves up and to seal ourselves off from others. Hetfield delivers the lyrics in second-person narration. He speaks to "you," but there can be no doubt that he is really chiding himself when he sings, "Struggle within / It suits you fine / Struggle within / Your ruin / Struggle within / You seal your own coffin." Ironically, these lines and this song are shared publicly. The very act of making and sharing art is a kind of therapy that can help break the shell of self, by confessing weaknesses and implicitly inviting help. Help might not be accepted, and the real nature of the struggle might not be admitted. However, it does seem like a chink in the defensive armor. The line consisting of the single word "hypocrite" is telling. The narrator wants to change, wants to break with old ways of doing and seeing things, yet he can't get himself to do it. He holds others responsible for their unwillingness to change and yet he finds himself hypocritically unwilling to change. The song starts with the lines "Reaching out for something you've got to feel / While clutching to what you had thought was real." The journey from the false to the true is not always straightforward, nor is it made in a single bound.

In "Escape" Hetfield had sung about breaking free from the chains that held him, but in "The Struggle Within" we see that the trap is more subtle and that the individual plays a key role in his own imprisonment. Growth and liberation require change, doing and trying new things. Such action requires making yourself uncomfortable, however. "So many things you don't want to do / What is it? What have you got to lose? / What the hell? / What is it you think you're gonna find? / Hypocrite / Boredom sets into the boring mind." In the past, "you" mocked your parents and others who were stuck in their ways and who were afraid to find the truth that new ways would reveal. Now you are similarly stuck yourself. The label you hurled at others, "hypocrite," has rebounded onto you. The morass in which you find yourself is loathsome and boring. Worse, you are boring. You have torn down the structures of a false reality, but you have not built anything positive and true to replace them.

It is hard not to read Hetfield's personal journey into the lyrics of "The Struggle Within." Hetfield had broken out of hell, the stifling false reality of his upbringing, and at the time of "The Struggle Within" he was an adult with a house of his own. But "Home is not a home, it becomes a hell / Turning it into your prison cell." A sort of selfish sense of control is glimpsed in the lines "Advantages are taken, not handed out / While you struggle inside your hell." The bombastic me-against-the-world pride expressed in "Escape" may have been necessary to break from the "true false world" but that tool, that attitude, turned against him both in his family and in his band. Indeed, by 1996 it turned him into "King Nothing," as the song from *Load* puts it.

In a searing self-portrait, Hetfield paints himself as lonely and alone like the fabled King Midas. What Hetfield touches may turn to gold records, but his insistence on control keeps people at arm's length. Depicting himself as "Hot and cold, bought and sold / A heart as hard as gold," Hetfield asks, "Are you satisfied?" The answer is obviously no. The insistence on control and dominion does not bring happiness but isolation. When everyone is forced to obey your commands, your life is loveless and lonely, especially when the falsity of the situation becomes apparent. People obey you out of fear, not love. As Hetfield sings, "Just want one thing / Just to play the king / But the castle's crumbled and you're left with just a name / Where's your crown / King Nothing?" Your castle is an illusion, just like your control over others. When your illusion is shattered, you see that all along you have only been playing at being the king. In reality, you're King Nothing, and no one wants to be near you: "Then it all crashes down / And you break your crown / And you point your finger / But there's no one around." You need other people, not just to obey you and do your bidding. You need to let them be who they are and to express themselves as they choose. Control over others is at best an illusion anyway. You may compel others to do as you wish, but you cannot control how they feel, nor ultimately would you want to. If you could control both the actions and the feelings of others, they would not be human—and you desperately want to have genuine relationships with other humans.

Upon the realization that you are King Nothing, the feeling of emptiness should be enough to catalyze a change. But unfortunately, self-knowledge is rarely sufficient to solve a problem. Admitting the problem is a necessary first step, but without making changes the problem will persist. And indeed the problem of exerting control over others continued to cause Hetfield pain, not to mention the pain he caused those around him. "All Within My Hands" from *St. Anger* continues the self-reflection on this theme. The song begins, "All within my hands / Squeeze it in, crush it down / All within my hands / Hold it dear, hold it suffocate." Here a newly sober Hetfield takes stock of some of the damage he has done to his family and his band. Metallica's bassist, Jason Newsted, had left the band in 2001, largely because Hetfield did not give Newsted enough creative input into the band and forbade Newsted and other members of Metallica from playing in other bands as side projects. As the documentary film *Metallica: Some Kind of Monster* reveals, Metallica very nearly broke up.

The album *St. Anger* is widely regarded as a musical low point for the band, but it was nonetheless a major achievement for Metallica to stay together and record new music. Under the direction of a therapist/coach, Phil Towle, the three remaining members of Metallica were urged to work more collaboratively. For the first time, on *St. Anger*, Hetfield did not write all the lyrics. There were other oddities as well. The band's producer, Bob Rock, played bass on the album but was not considered a member of the band. (After the recording, Metallica invited bassist Robert Trujillo to join the band.) The songs on *St. Anger* do not include guitar solos. Lead guitarist Kirk Hammett was thus marginalized, a strange occurrence for an album that was supposed to be made with a greater sense of collaboration. Another strange choice is the sound of Lars Ulrich's drums on *St. Anger*—the snare is deliberately out of tune. This is one case where it might have been beneficial for Hetfield to exert some influence and insist on a change. On the other hand, I personally like the drums on *St. Anger*. They sound broken, and that is fitting for the state of the band at the time. The drum sound and the piece-meal nature of the songs (such as the outro to "All Within My Hands") express a brokenness and an attempt to sew together disparate parts à la Frankenstein or "some kind of monster."

The line "Hold it dear, hold it suffocate" from "All Within My Hands" speaks volumes. It's as if Hetfield holds a fragile creature, a tiny bird or a newborn puppy. He realizes that he is doing it harm, but he can't bring himself to take the obvious and appropriate action of letting it go. Hetfield gets a rush from playing the role of protector: "Take your fear, pump me up." At first, the snare of his hands may seem safe and benevolent, but that appearance is false. He knows it too: "Trap all within my hands." Hetfield sings, "Love is control / I'll die if I let go." This seems to be a lesson Hetfield learned from his father. Virgil Hetfield was terribly controlling, but Hetfield knew that his father loved him. Both in his family and in his band, Hetfield repeated his father's mistake. Realization of the mistake bleeds into awareness with the admission that he is suffocating those he holds dear. Once again, self-knowledge is impotent on its own. The pain of giving up control and letting others act freely and uncoerced is chosen over the pain of letting go. The result is predictable to Hetfield and to everyone else. Despite wanting to do better, Hetfield knows he will not. With resignation he sings, "Kill all within my hands again." The line "Hate me now" echoes through the song. It's as if Hetfield is telling other people to cut to the chase and get it over with. You will not be able to endure my controlling ways, so go ahead and hate me now. Later in the song the line becomes "Hurry up and hate me now," emphasizing the inevitability. Of course, the line "Hate me now" may also be addressed to himself. He hates himself now, hates himself already, in the midst of his struggle, hates himself for suffocating others and being unable to let go of control.

The phrase "all within my hands" has a vaguely positive connotation, at least prior to hearing Hetfield's lyrics. The song's title might be taken to suggest a scenario in which a person has an opportunity to do good and bring about a positive outcome. Indeed in 2017 the band started a charitable organization and called it All Within My Hands. Among other things, the charity supports community colleges and fights homelessness. So it is within their hands to do good, and that is what one might expect upon first hearing the title of the song. But that notion is quickly dismissed as the chorus ends with a single word: "Beware."

Hetfield knows his pattern of behavior all too well. "I will only let you breathe / My air that you receive / Then we'll see if I let you love me." He has a warped sense of love. The master of puppets will play the role of protector and apparently grant freedom, but the liberty is illusory: "Let you run, then I pull your leash." You are under the control of someone who is not in control of himself. The chorus also includes the lyric "love to death." It's a phrase that people often use positively, as an indication of intensity and devotion, as in "I love her to death," without much awareness of how awful that really sounds. Hetfield gets it, though. He kills what he loves, perhaps not literally—but he realizes that loving someone or something "to death" is not a good thing. The cognitive dissonance rings in his head as he admits that for him, "control is love, love is control." He knows it's wrong, but he can't seem to find his way out, mainly because he is afraid to: "I'll die if I let go." Of course, he knows that he won't literally die, and at the end of the song, the line shifts subtly to "I'll fall if I let go." The fall would likewise not be literal, but it gets closer to the truth and the fear. Hetfield rose from the depths of being a shy kid in a struggling band to the heights of being the alpha male lead singer in one of the biggest bands in the world.

The seeds of being a controlling menace were sown in Hetfield's childhood thanks to the model of his father, but upbringing is not destiny. Hetfield was responsible for what he became, and he was, and is, responsible for undoing it. As he matured quickly into his role as front man for a great band that succeeded on its own terms, his creative genius and imposing physical presence naturally elicited respect. Not just respect but admiration and awe. I vividly recall seeing Hetfield standing outside his tour bus in the parking lot of the Meadowlands after the band opened for Ozzy Osbourne in 1986. I was 16 years old, and the 23-year-old Hetfield stood 15 feet away. The other members of the band were also briefly outside the tour bus. Cliff Burton was striking with his heavy metal hippie looks, but really it's as if the rest of the band and the crowd were in black and white while Hetfield was in color. Hetfield's scowling presence was a force felt at a distance. I've since been in the presence of other rock stars and celebrities, but I've never felt anything like that again. Of course, much of it may be due to my impressionable age at the time, but not all of it. Hetfield has changed quite a lot since then, but I suspect I would get a real sense of presence if I sat down with him today. I don't mean to suggest that there is something mystical or supernatural about him. Rather, much of what we communicate is nonverbal. In my recollection, the other members of the band, including Burton, were smiling. But Hetfield was scowling, and everything about his face and his posture shouted to me that he was the real thing—a guy who was truly hurt and damaged and truly raging against it and overcoming it. If other people experienced only a fraction of the force I felt from Hetfield, then it is no wonder that they were ready to play a subordinate role to him. Not only did he want control, but people wanted to give it to him. The ultimate result, though, was that he alienated the people he loved, afraid to take a fall from the alpha heights.

When the need for control is fed by success, it can generate the self-centeredness of the martyr and the savior. The attitude is that "only I can fix any situation. The rest of you need me but don't really appreciate me." "Atlas, Rise!" from the album *Hardwired . . . to Self-Destruct* depicts this self-constructed predicament. In Greek mythology, Atlas holds the world on his shoulders, and the song is structured with second-person narration: "How does it feel on your own? / Bound by the world all alone." The lyrics continue, "Crushed under heavy skies / Atlas, Rise!" Hetfield the narrator seems to be addressing himself, though perhaps a slightly younger version of himself. Maybe he has gotten some distance from thinking he is the great hero (or Titan god) on whom the weight of the world rests. He is telling the person he addresses to stop playing the role of martyr. Give it up. Share the burden. "All you bear / All you carry / All you bear / Place it right on, right on me." Atlas can rise and stand up straight only when he lets go of the weight of the world. In this case he will find that he was not really holding up the world anyway, or at least that the world can hold itself up without him. "My Friend of Misery" from The Black Album has a similar message—stop wallowing in your own self-pity. And the older song uses the same imagery in the lines "You insist that the weight of the world / Should be on your shoulders."

"Atlas, Rise!" begins by describing the unhappy state of a foolish figure, most likely Hetfield's former self or some part of his current self, or both. "Bitterness and burden / Curses rest on thee / Solitaire and sorrow / All Eternity." Atlas is not a happy servant. Rather, he is infected with resentment and woe, seeing his fate as lonely and burdensome. This makes sense. If you seize a task that could be shared, it is unlikely that others will appreciate you for it, especially if you take the task because you think that only you can do it well or properly. You "save the Earth and claim perfection." Acting the savior for those who don't seek a savior is a recipe for resentment: "Grudges break your back." It's not the weight of the work, but the lack of appreciation that makes the situation unbearable. And that is all your fault.

With an echo of Dylan, Hetfield asks, "How does it feel on your own?" Like the figure mocked in "Like a Rolling Stone," Hetfield's figure deserves his fate and must swallow his pride. Indeed, pride comes before the fall. Though he thought the role was real, Hetfield's figure has only been performing. He is not really a savior and has only been acting like a martyr—there is no cause that calls for his sacrifice. "Masquerade as maker," you're no god, no creator; you're just pretending, and you're fooling no one but yourself. The burden of being in charge is captured in the cliché "heavy is the head that wears the crown." In the song it becomes "heavy is the crown." Why? Perhaps because the burden of responsibility is false. Just as there literally is no crown in this case, there is no responsibility that you need to bear alone. The result is that "Beaten down and broken / Drama wears you down." It's not the weight of the world that causes your knees to buckle; it's the petty griping and backstabbing that causes you to fall. Hetfield chants the lyrics "Overload, the martyr stumbles /

Hit the ground and heaven crumbles / All alone, the fear shall humble / Swallow all your pride."

This Atlas has merely been holding up the skies. When this "martyr" falls, the earth doesn't fall; it's fine. Rather, "heaven crumbles." It's the false reality, the castle in the sky, that collapses. The result is that Atlas is humbled by fear and forced to swallow his pride. It is a more mature reaction than we get from King Nothing, who crashes down and points his finger in blame only to find no one around.

The subtlety and vulnerability of the emotions expressed in Hetfield's lyrics surprise some people. It is easy to think of him expressing anger and rage, but he paints sadness and fear with a deft palette. Indeed, "Atlas, Rise!" strikes a note of hope, an emotion not regularly associated with metal in general or Metallica in particular. The description of the death that awaits Atlas is at first grim: "Die as you suffer in vain." There is no point to what "you" are doing, no value in your suffering. But the next line is ambiguous: "Own all the grief and the pain." To "own" it might mean to take responsibility for it, in this case to take responsibility for the fact that you have caused your own grief and pain. What is the solution? You will "die as you hold up the skies." The imagery suggests the foolishness of the endeavor. The skies do not need to be held up. They never did. The "you" who will die from the weight of supporting the skies is the self-deceived and arrogant martyr. You must let "you" die. Only when that occurs can you become who you truly are. Only then can Atlas rise.

The imagery of death and rebirth is potent, as it implies that there is another chance. We can die to our old ways and become new. There is hope for even the most stubborn and close-minded among us. The weight of our own suffering can shake us out of the slumber of self-deception to see the world and ourselves as we truly are. To do that, though, we need other people. We need to share our suffering and burdens with them to lighten the load and clear the path. To do so does not diminish us. Atlas does not lose his identity or individuality. Instead, he is free to become strong and unburdened, as he is meant to be. He will not be completely independent, nor completely dependent. Instead, he will be interdependent, living with the mutual personal support that will allow him to thrive and become his best self.

# CHAPTER 10

# RESILIENCE

*Rise Again and Show Your Scars*

A tlas does not live happily ever after. No one does. When the rock star feeds on praise and adulation from fans and critics, he will sometimes go hungry. Many longtime Metallica fans were concerned about the commercial sound of The Black Album and bothered by the alternative sounds of *Load* and *Reload*. So, in 2003, *St. Anger* was greeted with eager anticipation of a return to a more original Metallica sound. Most fans were disappointed, though. *St. Anger* is heavy, and the title track, along with "Frantic," would belong on a greatest-hits compilation. Much of the album, though, is lumbering and uninspired. Of course, it was miraculous that the album was made at all, but the out-of-tune drums and absent guitar solos were enough for some fans, who had persisted through past disappointments, to finally throw in the towel.

To the pleasant surprise of many in 2008, *Death Magnetic* was one of the great comeback albums in rock history. Gone were the out-of-tune snare drums and back were Kirk Hammett's masterful guitar solos. The riffs and the tempo were a return to 1980s form. The lyrics reflect the fact that the negative fan reaction to past albums got to Hetfield. This is most explicit in "The Judas Kiss," where the imagery is a bit extreme. Judas is the ultimate turncoat, betraying Jesus with a kiss—his signal to the Romans that this is the man they are looking for. Judas is the quintessential false friend, who does not stick with you when times are tough and actually goes over to the other side. And Jesus is . . . well, God, at least according to the story. So Hetfield's imagery is unfair to fans and a bit too flattering to himself. Hetfield is not God, though some fans, including me, may have claimed that he was sometimes. More importantly, the fans were not Judas. Fans don't owe unceasing devotion to bands. Musicians are free to change styles, and fans are free to dislike the new styles and stop buying albums and going to concerts. Fans are even free to vocally ridicule the new music without being labeled traitors. So Hetfield is grandiose in his imagery, but the grandiosity is appropriate for capturing the depth of his feelings. And to his credit, in "The Judas Kiss" he is not pretending that he is bulletproof and impervious to criticism. Contrast that with the silly lyrics of "Shoot Me Again" from *St. Anger*, inspired by Lars Ulrich's response to the fan backlash against Metallica's opposition to Napster: "I won't go away, with a bullet in my back / Right here I'll stay, with a bullet in my back."

Instead of a bullet in his back, the narrator of "The Judas Kiss" has a different experience: "When the world has turned its back / When the days have turned pitch black." Gone is the hot bravado, replaced by a cold vulnerability. To him, it feels like not just a few fans or critics are taking pot shots, but rather that the whole world has ceased to care. Instead of the red-hot anger of the previous album, we get the pitch-black despair of being left for dead. The narrator's response is emotional paralysis, as he describes what happens "When the fear abducts your tongue / When the fire's dead and gone." Here Hetfield is emotionally honest with the admission that he is not above, or impervious to, fans or critics. Rather, he is subject to self-doubt. Could he write a new song that was true to his current artistic vision and that fans would appreciate? The state in which "fear abducts your tongue" sounds like writer's block in which nothing comes out, as in some nightmare when you find you cannot speak. Worse, though, is the situation in which "the fire's dead and gone."

The public face of the band—mostly Lars Ulrich in interviews, but sometimes Hetfield and others—never really admitted to feeling hurt by fans who felt betrayed by the band. But now in this song, "The Judas Kiss," it becomes clear that the fans were not the only ones who felt betrayed. Hetfield did too. Not only did it upset and anger him, it filled him with fear. Fear, though, can be channeled and used creatively. The real problem is that the fire in the belly, the will to fight, seemed gone, at least momentarily. Hetfield describes it as the moment "when you think it's all said and done." There is no more fight within you, no vision for sublimating anger or fear, nothing. You are a boxer down for the count; you are ready to admit defeat. When the crowd is cheering for the boxer to get up, he may muster the fortitude to rise and go once more into the fray, but when the crowd is celebrating his fall to the canvas and his strength is depleted, it is tempting to give up and stay down.

If you are Hetfield, you have built a legion of fans, but now they no longer want their leader; "you are the ostracized." The irony is rich because you have been the tastemaker in the past, cocreating thrash metal and reviving interest in The Misfits and the new wave of British heavy metal. Now you are no longer cool;

you are a hack and a has-been, a boxer who stayed too long in the ring. You can't avoid reading the "selfish ridden dead goodbyes." Fans and critics have written you off. The word "ridden" sounds like "written" when Hetfield sings it, and several unofficial lyrics websites have the phrase as "selfish *written* dead goodbyes," which might make more sense. The "dead goodbyes" are the premature (as it turns out) musical obituaries for the band. Calling them "selfish written" could imply that they are composed in a selfish and mean-spirited way. The official lyric "selfish ridden" (like moth-ridden) would imply that the "dead goodbyes" are infested with selfishness. By contrast, an obituary or eulogy is ordinarily an occasion for generosity, kindness, and praise. The result of being "ostracized" and forced to read "dead goodbyes" is that you are left "Twisting on the tourniquet / When the pieces never fit." A tourniquet slows the flow of blood through a vein or artery, and it is often used as a lifesaving device. The imagery suggests the seriousness of the situation. It is as if he may bleed to death from the wounds inflicted by being "ostracized" and forced to read "dead goodbyes."

What may be worse is that he can't make sense of the situation or how to fix it; "the pieces never fit" and a tourniquet is only a temporary way to keep him alive. When a solution is readily apparent, it can be easy to take action. However, when the situation shows itself as a puzzle in which the pieces do not fit, the result is confusion, inaction, and a sense of defeat. Self-deception may explain why the pieces don't fit. For a long time, "you" have been kidding yourself about the effects of criticism, but when the blinders are finally pulled away, the experience is overwhelming and disorienting. The result is an existential crisis in which the world ceases to make sense. The truth, though, is that the world remains the same as it has always been. It is just that the order and interpretation you have imposed on the world no longer holds. The human mind seeks order and finds it even in places where there is no real order, in cloud patterns, inkblots, and sometimes in song lyrics. With its days that "have turned pitch black," the song shows a despairing response to the loss of order and meaning. Not only is the past order lost, but the narrator despairs at the possibility of constructing a new one.

Some self-reference to the songwriting process may be in play here. The lyricist chooses the words, but he must make them fit the song. As a result, he must sometimes say what he wants indirectly and imperfectly. "The Judas Kiss" has moments of brilliance in making the words and the meaning fit, but the song shows its seams where the narrator seems to change, and the narrative flow seems disrupted in the verses that begin "Bow down" and "Followed you from dawn of time." Ultimately, it feels like two or more songs have been sewn together. Maybe I'm wrong about that, though. If the job of the songwriter is to make the pieces fit, then the job of the interpreter is to explain how they do. The songwriter may try to get away with pieces that don't fit, and the interpreter may discover ways they go together that were not intended by the songwriter.

Regardless of the song's disjointed nature, "The Judas Kiss" packs an emotional punch, depicting the pit of despair in which the world no longer makes sense. The floor has been ripped out from under you or the card castle has tumbled down around you. The energy and intensity of the song suggest that one should not wallow in the despair, no matter how dark and heavy it may be. In fact, of course, the song itself is a creative reaction to that despair. As noted, though, the lyrics don't show the way up and out. The song simply suggests that "when you think it's all said and done," it's not—you need to fight your way back.

Another song from *Death Magnetic*, "Broken, Beat & Scarred," provides the lyrical response to the plight of "The Judas Kiss." The situation is universal, or as nearly universal as anything is in human experience. You are down and defeated and you are tempted to give up. "The Judas Kiss" depicts a particular instance of this experience, but whatever the cause, the response must be the same: rise again. With the lines "Through black days / Through black nights / Through pitch black insides," the song "Broken, Beat & Scarred" seems to be describing the state of despair in "The Judas Kiss." Here, though, the pieces of the puzzle begin to fit. The solution that was missing from "The Judas Kiss" is provided in the repeated call to "rise again." The human condition is such that you must "rise, fall, down, rise again." Of course, not everyone does rise again. Some people fall and stay down. Others rise multiple times but eventually rise no more. A Japanese proverb instructs, "Fall down seven times, get up eight." This is the key to success. It is not how many times you fail or how badly you are defeated, but how many times you regroup and try again.

Something more than mere resilience is possible. Repackaging a line from Nietzsche, Hetfield sings, "What don't kill ya make ya more strong." With resilience, one bounces back as good as new. But if one is only as good as before, there may not be much reason to think that things will be different this time. The key is to become better and stronger. Nassim Taleb captures this Nietzschean concept with the term "antifragile." Things that are fragile break under pressure, whereas things that are resilient bounce back to their previous state. But things that are antifragile actually get better and improve after suffering pressures or shocks. In many cases the human body is antifragile—not only does it bounce back after a disease, but it is often better and stronger because it now has antibodies to prevent the disease the next time. Muscles are antifragile: when torn down by exercise, they rebuild and become stronger.

It can sound like silly macho talk to invoke the Nietzschean line à la Hetfield, claiming that "what don't kill ya make ya more strong," but it is an ideal to aspire towards. Rather than accept defeat and stay down, you can muster the fortitude to rise again. This is not a matter of being a resilient punching bag or a Whac-A-Mole. It takes time. The image of the phoenix comes to mind. The fire bird turns to ash, seeming dead and gone, but then it roars back. Rising again takes patience, not just determination. For all its glory and inspiration, the phoenix is not antifragile. It is simply, though supremely, resilient. Unlike the bird, the person who rises again is made antifragile through experience. Vaccines work on the principle of antifragility, giving us a small dose of the disease in order to stimulate antibodies and develop immunity. Likewise, the experience of rising after defeat or failure provides confidence and a blueprint for how to do it the next time. This is not your first rodeo—you've been thrown from a bucking bronco before. Every situation is different, but you can generalize from your experience to find the confidence to rise again. It's not clear if antifragility is a skill that can be taught. If it is, then few skills could be more valuable, and it should be taught from a young age. What is clear, though, is that antifragility can be modeled. We can learn it from observing others, even if we can't learn it from an instruction book. Since it can be modeled, we have a duty to be honest with others. We should not pretend that we are unharmed by the "slings and arrows of outrageous fortune" and "the thousand natural shocks that flesh is heir to."

Less poetic than the bard, but no less wounded, Hetfield intones, "They scratch me / They scrape me / They cut and rape me." At first the imagery of scratches and scrapes calls to mind

**THE MEANING OF METALLICA**

the death by a thousand paper cuts or the straw that breaks the camel's back, the regular injuries and insults to which we are all subject and under whose weight we sometimes buckle and fall. But then the imagery becomes more severe and serious with the cut and the rape, injuries that leave physical and emotional scars. We all suffer these as well, though not all of us literally in the case of rape. Perhaps we should not speak figuratively of rape, but there is an archaic sense of the word in which it does not necessarily involve intercourse and simply means to seize and take away by force. It is the sense of being violated, even if not sexually, of having something ripped away from us, that is common to human experience. Our instinct is often to cover our wounds, even to deny that they are there, or at least to pretend that they have healed and no longer bother us. The power of Hetfield's song derives not just from mighty guitar riffs but from its message that we should not conceal our psychological injuries. We incur them in the midst of daily life and should proudly display them for the world to see. "Breaking your teeth on the hard life comin' / Show your scars / Cutting your feet on the hard earth runnin' / Show your scars / Bleeding your soul in a hard luck story / Show your scars / Spilling your blood in the hot sun's glory / Show your scars." Of course, scars can be used to impress and intimidate others, but that is not the intention in this case. Rather, the intention is to take pride in a way that simultaneously salutes your individual toughness and recognizes our common humanity. Yes, your scars, emotional or physical, are badges of honor, but they are also indications of vulnerability. Thus we display toughness not in pretending to be bulletproof but in admitting that we bleed as easily as anyone else.

"Broken, Beat & Scarred" begins in the second person— "You rise / You fall"—but it feels as if Hetfield is speaking of his own experience. This perspective becomes clear when he switches to the first person as the object: "They scratch me." By the middle of the song, though, the second person is directed to the listener with the imperative to "show your scars." By the final line of the song, the narrator and the listener are joined in common cause in the first-person plural "we die hard." There is no yielding softness in the face of death or defeat. We don't give up easily. The message is not just a command but a wish and a reminder. If we are not literally killed, then we have a chance to rise again, to re-create ourselves as something better and stronger. Ultimately, we are all engaged in "the fight to the final breath." With death disappears the chance to become stronger. We may rise again in another form, but who knows what awaits us in "the undiscovered country, from whose bourn / No traveller returns"?

# CONCLUSION

# "THIS SEARCH GOES ON"

**N**early every Metallica song is someone's favorite, and it's special to that person in a way I wouldn't be able to capture. So this book has not examined every song in the Metallica catalog, but did you really think there would be an in-depth discussion of the lyrics for "Fuel"? Not all songs are created equal. Still, I would love to hear from you about your favorites. Here are my e-mail address and Twitter handle again: williamirwin@kings.edu and @williamirwin38. Tell me what I missed. Tell me what I got wrong. Tell me what Metallica means to you.

Thankfully, Metallica is not done. "This search goes on." More Metallica songs will be coming our way, even if new music takes longer than we'd like. For me, each new album is a chance to be with an old friend again. My friend and I have both been worn and weathered by the passage of time, but a strong bond puts us right back on the same wavelength. My friend will start a story that sounds familiar, but just when I think, "I've heard this one before," it will go in a surprising direction. Sometimes my friend and I like the changes we find in each other, and sometimes we don't. Some reunions spark joy and nostalgia. Others don't. Maybe our expectations are too high or pointed in the wrong direction, but we appreciate each meeting as a bridge between our past and our future.

James Hetfield's renewed sobriety and the chaotic state of our world will certainly influence the lyrical direction of new songs. Whatever changes and developments occur, Metallica's music will continue to inspire us to rise and meet the challenges we face. And as long as Cthulhu doesn't emerge from the depths, there will be hope for humanity.

# ACKNOWLEDGMENTS

I n the 1980s I spent countless hours with record albums, not just listening to the music but also staring at the cover art, reading the lyrics on the sleeves, and studying the liner notes. I didn't become a rock star, so these acknowledgments are the closest I'll ever come to having liner notes on an album.

Big Metalli-thanks to all those who helped make this book a reality. My wife, Megan Lloyd, read an early draft of the book manuscript and made great suggestions for stylistic improvements. Megan is not a Metallica fan, so that's real love! Joanna Corwin is a Metallica fan, one of the most devoted there is. She's also a great reader and friend. Joanna offered invaluable feedback on the manuscript that helped me to restructure the book. Likewise, Jason Eberl offered astute comments on the whole manuscript that improved the finished product greatly. Ben Hamilton read the first two chapters and offered much-needed encouragement at a time when I wasn't sure if the book would work. Elektra D. Mercutio similarly offered support.

Mark White and Jeff Dean gave great feedback on the book proposal that eventually led to a contract. Greg Renoff, whose books on Van Halen and Ted Templeman I admire, connected me with the publisher, ECW, and my editor, Michael Holmes— who is also a Metallica fan. How cool is that? Peter Norman and Adrineh Der-Boghossian expertly copyedited and proofread the manuscript, saving me from hitting some duff notes. Shannon Parr guided the manuscript and me along the winding path to publication. Brie Gentry and Matt Bridges were instrumental in securing permission to quote the lyrics of Metallica.

King's College granted me a sabbatical to write this book, among other things. I am fortunate to work at a place that has supported my eccentric ways. My King's colleagues Mike Church and Charlie Brooks are responsible for the concept of subtle suicide (subtlesuicide.com), which I discuss in the book. *Psychology Today* deserves thanks for allowing me to try out words and ideas, including some about Metallica, on its blog.

Over the years, many friends (too many to list) have listened to me ramble and pontificate about Metallica. I can't thank you enough for your patience and for your own insights. I learned much about Metallica from the various authors who contributed to a previous book I edited, *Metallica and Philosophy: A Crash Course in Brain Surgery*. Truly, I wish to thank everyone who has written about and interviewed Metallica. I've read more than I can recall, but among the best books on the subject are: *Birth School Metallica Death: The Inside Story of Metallica (1981–1991)* and *Into the Black: The Inside Story of Metallica (1991–2014)*, both by Paul Brannigan and Ian Winwood; *Metallica: The Frayed Ends of Metal*, by Chris Crocker; *Metallica Unbound: The Unofficial Biography*, by K.J. Doughton; *So Let It Be Written: The Biography of Metallica's James Hetfield*, by Mark Eglinton; *Metallica: The*

*Stories Behind the Songs*, by Chris Ingham; *Metallica*, by David Masciotra; *Justice for All: The Truth about Metallica* and *To Live Is to Die: The Life and Death of Metallica's Cliff Burton*, both by Joel McIver; and *Enter Night: A Biography of Metallica*, by Mick Wall.

Last and most of all, thanks to Metallica for providing the soundtrack of my life, and especially to James Hetfield for lyrics that light the way in dark times.